Happiness Dissected

Mark Devon

www.happinessdissected.com

www.happinessdissected.com

ISBN: 1514637472
ISBN-13: 978-1514637470

August 6, 2015

Table of Contents

Table of Contents

Chapter 1
Introduction

When you're happy, you feel a positive emotion. When you're unhappy, you feel a negative emotion. This book dissects happiness into these individual emotions based on their unique evolutionary or biological purpose.

This dissection reveals many breakthrough insights, such as:

- you only fall in love with strangers
- women only fall in love with men of equal-or-higher rank
- men fall out of love 4 years after meeting a woman
- you only envy former peers – like siblings and classmates
- you only feel humor when others make a mistake that you could make
- a mid-life crisis occurs when your rank plateaus and you stop feeling pride
- we say please and thank you so others don't feel humiliation
- we only cry because we're lonely

This book builds on *The Origin of Emotions* – the first book to identify the purpose, trigger and effect of each emotion. While *The Origin of Emotions* explains the theoretical rationale for each emotion's purpose and function, *Happiness Dissected* explains how each emotion affects happiness – yours and those around you.

This book examines anything that makes you feel a positive or negative mental effect. In addition to emotions like love or jealousy, it also examines sensations, like sexual pleasure or pleasing taste, which also make you feel a positive or negative mental effect.

www.happinessdissected.com

www.theoriginofemotions.com

Chapter 2
Monogynic Love

Men feel monogynic love when they fall in love.
Men feel monogynic love when their woman is happy. And the happier she is, the stronger the love they feel.

Monogynic love ties a man's happiness directly to his woman's happiness. If she's happy, he's happy. If she's not happy, he's not happy. This effectively turns men into happy slaves to their women – while they're in love.

Monogynic love helps a man's genes indirectly by encouraging him to support the mother of his children. By comparison, maternal love helps a woman's genes directly by encouraging her to care for her children. This combination of emotions ensures that children have two-parent, conflict-free, post-natal care.

Men can only fall in love with strangers.
Said alternatively, men cannot fall in love with women they've known for more than a few months – like friends or old flames. This feature of monogynic love encourages men to have each child with a different woman.

Having each child with a different woman maximizes a man's long run reproduction by maximizing the genetic diversity of his offspring. It avoids committing all of his children to a bad mutation that leaves his genes on a dead-end street. And it maximizes the chances of producing at least one child with a good mutation that becomes a necessary bridge to the future.

A man who wants to fall in love should enter new social circles – where all of the women will be strangers to him. A woman who wants a man to fall in love with her should also enter new social circles – where she will be a stranger to all of the men.

Men fall in love after 4 months – if two things occur during those 4 months.
First, the woman must show an hourglass figure. She doesn't need a perfect figure. And she doesn't need to be nude or wear a bikini. She only needs to show a clothed silhouette that has the basic outline of an hourglass figure.

Second, she must interact at least 40 hours a week with the man. The interaction must involve eye contact, smiling and talking. Texting, emails and social networking do not count.

Both requirements help avoid the worst case scenario for a man's genes – falling in love with a woman who is pregnant with another man's child. Showing an hourglass figure for 4 months proves that a woman wasn't impregnated by another man just before they met – if she had been, she would show by month 4 and lose her hourglass figure. Interacting 40 hours a week makes it unlikely a woman had the time to be courted and impregnated by another man since they met.

Men don't need to have sex with a woman to fall in love with her. Having sex helps because it shows a woman's hourglass figure and involves face-to-face interaction. However, having dinner in the right dress has the same effect as having sex.

Men can only love one woman at a time – hence the label monogynic.
This means men will be socially monogamous, but it doesn't mean they'll be sexually monogamous. While men in love focus their support on one woman, they may still cheat sexually.

However, men in love are more reluctant to cheat than men who have fallen out of love. If a man in love is caught, his woman will be unhappy which stops him feeling love. If a man who has fallen out of love is caught, his woman will be unhappy but it doesn't stop him feeling love – he wasn't in love.

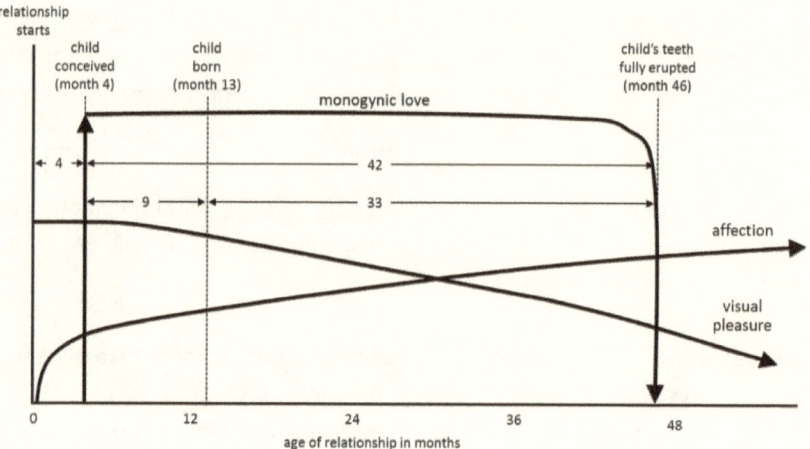

Men fall out of love 46 months after meeting a woman – almost 4 years.
Men fall in love 4 months after meeting a woman and fall out of love 42 months later. Adding the 4 months required to fall in love to the 42 months of monogynic love means that men fall out of love 46 months after meeting a woman – almost 4 years.

Men only love a woman for 42 months because that supports a woman through 9 months of pregnancy and 33 months of post-natal care – when a child's first set of teeth have fully erupted.

In the past, a child needed two parents to eat until its first set of teeth had fully erupted. Before we had baby formula and Gerber food, mothers fed their children through breastfeeding and mouth-to-mouth transfer of masticated food. Feeding children was a full-time job for mother and supporting mothers was a full-time job for fathers.

Once a child's first set of teeth have fully erupted, things change. With all of their teeth, children can eat if given food. They no longer need the full-time care of two parents – they can be managed part-time by one adult watching multiple children. That frees parents to move on to the next child. To encourage men to move on to the next woman when a child's teeth have fully erupted, monogynic love for the current woman stops after 42 months or 46 months after meeting her – almost 4 years.

8

After 4 years with a woman, men do continue to feel the weaker positive sensations of affection and visual pleasure when they see their woman. These sensations are usually mistaken as weaker forms of love.

Affection is a positive sensation we all feel when we see or hear a familiar person – see Chapter 6. The more familiar somebody is to you, the stronger the affection you feel when you see or hear them. After 4 years of being together, a couple will make each other feel moderately strong affection. When people say they love each other, they usually mean they feel affection.

Visual pleasure is a positive sensation men feel when they see women – see Chapter 24. The visual pleasure that a man feels looking at a particular woman is strongest when he first sees her. It then continually declines over time as she loses her novelty. After 4 years, even a supermodel will only make her man feel weak visual pleasure.

After 4 years, men are no longer motivated to make their woman happy.
While men are in love, love rewards them for making their woman happy. After they fall out of love, affection and visual pleasure just reward men for being with their woman – whether she is happy or not. After 4 years, men change from happy slaves to indifferent roommates.

Men should expect to fall out of love after 4 years.
Men's happiness will noticeably decline 4 years after meeting a woman. Men should not attribute their loss of happiness to some other issue and then mistakenly change that other issue. They should not, for example, blame their career and change jobs. More importantly, they should not blame the woman they loved. It doesn't matter who she is or what she did, they would've stopped loving her after 4 years. No woman makes a man feel love forever.

Men can feel love again with a new woman. However, they'll end up in the same situation 4 years later. And they'll only feel the moderate affection that a 4 year relationship makes you feel. If a man stays with one woman after he falls out of love, he'll feel the stronger affection that an 8 year or more relationship makes you feel.

Chapter 3
Infatuation

monogynic love	infatuation
men feel it when their woman is happy	women feel it when men think they are sexy

When women "fall in love", they feel infatuation – not love.

The romantic emotions of the two genders differ as much as their genitalia. While both genders feel a strong positive emotion when they fall in love, their romantic emotions evolved for very different purposes. While monogynic love encourages men to support a woman, the positive emotion that women feel encourages them to attract the sexual interest of men. To recognize this gender difference, the emotion women feel is called infatuation – not love.

To put it simply, men feel love when their woman is happy and women feel infatuation when men think they are sexy. The difference is reflected in their behavior. Men in love spend money to make their women happy – buying presents for their women, for example. Infatuated women spend money to make themselves attractive to their man – buying clothes for themselves, for example.

Women don't need to love men. Children would not gain if mothers loved fathers – monogynic love already glues fathers to mothers.

Women do need to make men fall in love – which is the purpose of infatuation. Men fall in love after seeing an hourglass figure and having frequent interaction for 4 months. Infatuation rewards women for attracting a man's sexual interest – which is best done by showing him an hourglass figure. And frequently attracting a man's sexual interest leads to frequent interaction. While love turns men into happy slaves, infatuation turns women into attention seekers.

Women can only become infatuated with strangers.
Said alternatively, women cannot become infatuated with men they've known for more than a few months – like friends or old flames. This feature encourages women to have each child with a different man. Both genders maximize reproduction by maximizing the genetic diversity of their offspring.

Romance writers understand that women can only become infatuated with strangers. Their novels always focus on a tall, dark stranger.

A woman who wants to become infatuated should enter new social circles – where all of the men will be strangers to her. A man who wants a woman to become infatuated with him should also enter new social circles – where he will be a stranger to all of the women.

Women can only become infatuated with men of equal-or-higher rank.
If a woman believes a man is lower rank than her, he will never make her feel infatuation. A working woman, for example, will never feel infatuation from the attention of an unemployed man. A supermodel, for example, will not feel infatuation when construction workers whistle at her – but a schoolgirl will.

The equal-or-higher rank feature ensured the evolution of ambition in humans. It gives ambitious men an advantage by eliminating unambitious men from the competition for a woman's attention.

Without this advantage, ambitious men would have fewer children than unambitious men. Ambitious men spend more hours striving to improve their rank and fewer hours in courtship. And fewer hours spent in courtship translates into fewer children. If ambitious men have fewer children than unambitious men, eventually ambitious people will go extinct.

With this advantage, ambitious men are more successful per hour of courtship because they face fewer competitors. This offsets the fewer hours they spend in courtship. Consequently, ambitious men have the same number of successful courtships as unambitious men – and the same number of children.

To be more accurate, this advantage <u>ensured the evolution of the emotions</u> <u>that motivate people to be ambitious</u> – the four rank emotions:

- pride
- humiliation
- envy
- humor

To be even more accurate, this advantage <u>ensured the evolution of all group</u> <u>emotions</u>. In addition to the four rank emotions, group emotions include:

- revenge
- criminal guilt
- compassion
- selfish guilt
- excitement
- boredom

Consequently, infatuation makes women prefer men who <u>display behavior</u> <u>motivated by group emotions</u> – not just ambition. For example, women also prefer men who are funny (humor), macho (revenge), law-abiding (criminal guilt), heroic (compassion), charitable (selfish guilt) or adventurous (excitement).

<u>For simplicity, "rank" = "display behavior motivated by group emotions".</u>
Instead of stating, for example, that "women can only become infatuated with <u>men who display behavior motivated by group emotions as much as they do</u>", the book will continue to state that "women can only become infatuated with <u>men of equal-or-higher-rank</u>".

Rank is a good proxy for group emotions for two reasons. First, the most important group emotions are the rank emotions – pride, humiliation, envy and humor. The higher your rank is, the more rank emotions motivate you. Second, the other group emotions encourage impulsive behavior which is a small fraction of total behavior. Compassion, for example, encourages people to be heroic in tragedies, which are brief and rare. Envy, by comparison, encourages people to work long hours for years trying to match a peer.

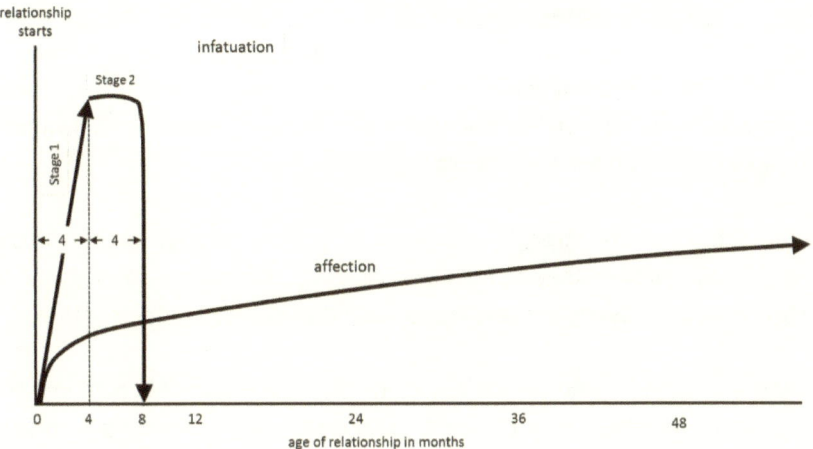

For any one man, infatuation has an 8 month cycle with two 4 month stages.
The two stages evolved for different purposes. The first stage rewards women for making a man fall in love. The second stage rewards women for conceiving a child with that man.

Stage 1: infatuation grows stronger if one man makes a woman feel it daily.
If, for example, a man watches a woman as she walks by every day, he'll make her feel slightly stronger infatuation each day she walks by.   If a man compliments a female co-worker about her looks every day, he'll make her feel slightly stronger infatuation each time he compliments her. Contact frequency doesn't have to be every single day to cause infatuation to grow stronger. It can be just five days a week and infatuation will still grow stronger.

This feature encourages women to focus their sexual appeal on one man. Women can feel infatuation from multiple men at the same time, but they will increasingly focus on the man who makes them feel the strongest infatuation. As women focus their sex appeal on one man, they do what makes him fall in love: show him an hourglass figure and have frequent interaction.

Stage 1 is 4 months long because it takes 4 months for men to fall in love. As discussed in the previous chapter, a woman who maintains an hourglass figure for 4 months could not have been impregnated by another man just before the relationship began.

Stage 2: infatuation plateaus and sexual pleasure is temporarily elevated.

Stage 2 doesn't begin unless a woman has just experienced 4 months of growing infatuation from one man. This ensures that a woman doesn't move to stage 2 unless the man has fallen in love – which he would have if a woman has just experienced 4 months of growing infatuation.

During this stage, the strength of infatuation plateaus at very strong. This is when women believe they have "fallen in love". Infatuation stays strong to keep a woman focussing her sexual appeal on the man for 4 more months.

During this stage, women enjoy sex more than usual. Vaginal pleasure and lubrication are temporarily elevated. Elevating sexual pleasure encourages women to mate with their man <u>now</u>. He has just fallen in love and will therefore happily provide 42 months of support.

This stage stops after 4 months because that provides three ovulatory cycles to conceive a child. If a man cannot impregnate a woman after three cycles, he probably never will. If he cannot impregnate her, she should move on to a man who can.

Women reach stage 2 quicker with higher-ranking men.

As stated earlier in this chapter, women can only become infatuated with men of equal-or-higher rank. Among those men of equal-or-higher rank, the higher a man's rank, the stronger the infatuation a woman feels during stage 1. Movie stars, for example, make women feel stronger infatuation than regular men.

Because they make women feel stronger infatuation, higher-ranking men also reach the stage 2 plateau sooner. While a man of equal rank will take 4 months to reach stage 2, a higher-ranking man may only need 3 months. A movie star may only need a week.

This is another advantage given to higher-ranking men to ensure the evolution of ambition. This advantage shortens the time required to complete courtship for ambitious men. This also helps offset the fact that they spend less total time in courtship than unambitious men.

After 8 months of infatuation, women feel three changes.

First, their happiness drops like a step. They suddenly stop feeling the strong positive effect of infatuation they've felt for 8 months – the fireworks end. They continue to feel affection when they see or hear their man, but it's much weaker than infatuation.

Second, women's motivation changes. They're no longer motivated by infatuation to be sexually appealing to their man. Instead, they're only motivated by affection to simply be with their man. Consequently, they increasingly dress to be comfortable around their man – not to be sexually appealing. They are, however, still motivated by infatuation to be sexually appealing to other men – and they still dress to be sexually appealing around other men.

Third, women's sexual pleasure is no longer elevated. Vaginal pleasure and lubrication return to normal until the next time a man causes infatuation to reach stage 2. For women, sex goes back to being a chore.

Women can only become infatuated with a man once.

As previously stated, women can only become infatuated with a stranger. Men that have previously made a woman feel infatuation are obviously not strangers anymore and therefore cannot make her feel infatuation again.

It's important for women to remember this when deciding whether to continue a relationship. Women can never return to the romantic fireworks they once felt for a man. Once infatuation has completed its 8 month cycle for a particular man, a woman can only feel the weaker emotion of affection. Women thinking about continuing a relationship should assume no more fireworks – just slowly growing affection.

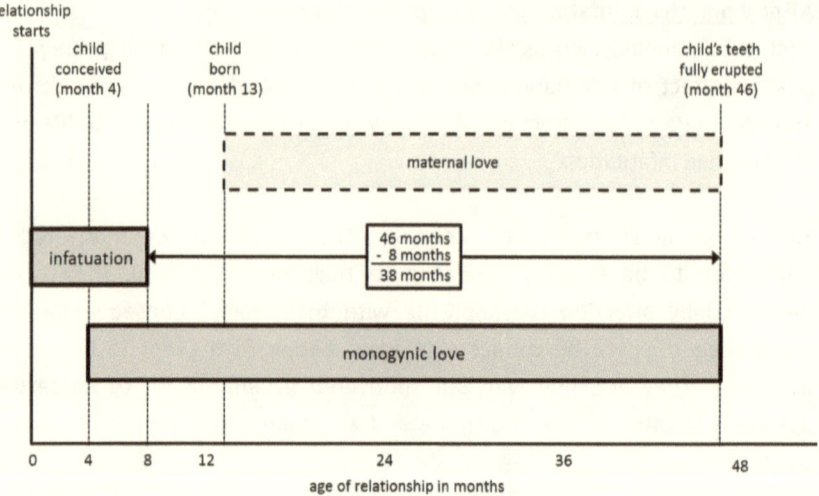

Childless women face a 38 month gap when infatuation ends.

Although women stop feeling infatuation after month 8, men continue to feel monogynic love until month 46 of a relationship. In childless relationships, this leaves a 38 month gap where men are happy but women are not. (If women have a child, they feel maternal love.)

If women expect this 38 month gap, they're less likely to blame their lost happiness on the wrong cause and apply the wrong remedy. They're, for example, less likely to blame their career and switch jobs. And they're less likely to blame their man. They would've felt less happy when their infatuation ended regardless of who their man was or what he did.

During the 38 month gap, women often push for children or marriage. They hope to replace their lost infatuation with maternal love or pride. A child will make them feel maternal love. A ring and a wedding will make them feel pride.

During the 38 month gap, women often flirt with other men and make their man jealous. Since women in the gap cannot feel infatuation from their man, they seek it from other men. And since their man is still in love with them, he feels jealousy when they flirt. This combination can quickly lead to a bad relationship or breakup. See the next chapter for more on jealousy.

During the 38 month gap, women often leave men. They hope to replace their lost infatuation by becoming infatuated with a new man. Famous women, who can easily find new men, tend to use this approach. Taylor Swift, for example, seems to have a new man every 12 months.

Women who stay enjoy growing affection. The longer you have been with someone, the stronger the affection they make you feel. Women who change relationships frequently do not enjoy this growing affection. They only feel weak affection from their men because they have only known their men for a few years.

Post-menopausal women do not feel infatuation.

Menopause evolved to encourage women to focus childcare on the next generation – their grandchildren. In addition to no longer ovulating, women's emotions change. They stop feeling maternal love and infatuation. And they start feeling grandmaternal love.

Post-menopausal women continue to dress attractively after menopause, but their motivation changes. Before menopause, a key reason for dressing attractively was to catch the attention of men and feel infatuation. After menopause, women only dress attractively to elevate their rank and feel pride. The brand of clothes they are wearing becomes more important than its ability to turn a man's head. Handbags become more important than lingerie.

Gay relationships are most stable. Lesbian relationships are least stable.

Gay relationships are two men feeling monogynic love for almost 4 years. And love motivates both partners to make the other partner happy.

By comparison, lesbian relationships are two women feeling infatuation for just 8 months. And infatuation only motivates both partners to attract the sexual interest of the other – not to make the other partner happy.

Heterosexual relationships are midway between gay and lesbian relationships. Men feel monogynic love for almost 4 years, but women only feel infatuation for 8 months. Men are motivated to make women happy, but women are only motivated to attract men's sexual interest – not to make him happy.

Chapter 4
Jealousy

Men start feeling jealousy when their women cheat or just flirt.
Men start feeling the negative effect of jealousy when they learn their woman has made another man feel sexual pleasure of any kind – penile or visual. Men obviously get jealous if another man has sex with their woman. But they also get jealous if another man just enjoys looking at their woman. Flirting is not harmless fun – it's painful for men.

Jealousy helps prevent the worst case scenario for a man's genes – raising another man's child. To prevent this scenario, a man must prevent courtship with another man escalating to intercourse. To prevent this escalation, men are coerced by jealousy to react to any courtship – including just flirting.

The more pleasure the other man feels, the stronger jealousy feels.
A man will feel weak jealousy if another man just enjoys looking at his woman. A man will feel much stronger jealousy if another man has sex with his woman.

This is why jealous men want to know the details of what a woman did with another man. They want to hear that it was only flirting which will only make them feel weak jealousy. They don't want to hear that the other man enjoyed fellatio which will make them feel very strong jealousy.

Jealousy gets stronger to match the threat. The more advanced a woman's cheating, the more pressure jealousy puts on a man to intervene.

Men stop feeling jealousy when they punish their women.
Men stop feeling jealousy when they have punished their woman equal to the sexual pleasure she made another man feel – a punishment-for-pleasure variation of the eye-for-an-eye theme of revenge – see Chapter 12. If a woman flirted with another man, for example, a jealous man can probably stop his jealousy by just yelling at her. If she fellated another man, he may need to be violent to stop his jealousy.

This matching of punishment-for-pleasure ensures that men don't harm their women more than necessary. Most threats can be stopped at the flirtation stage with a mild rebuke – which does not cause any serious injury.

Jealous men often harm the other man when they learn of cheating. However, this is mostly driven by the mistaken belief that harming the other man will stop jealousy. It won't unless it also bothers the woman. If she is distressed by seeing her other man harmed, then it will punish her indirectly. However, jealousy is best stopped by punishing the woman directly.

Men can only feel jealousy while they're in love.
Men can only feel jealousy from month 4 to month 46 of a relationship.

Women intuitively know that men only feel jealousy while they're in love. Women will flirt with other men just to see if it makes their man jealous. If the relationship has just started, the appearance of jealousy confirms that a man has fallen in love. If the relationship is more than 4 years old, the absence of jealousy confirms that a man has fallen out love.

Chapter 5
Heartbreak

jealousy	heartbreak
men feel it when women make another man feel sexual pleasure	women feel it when men fall in love with another woman
men stop feeling it when they punish women	women never stop feeling it

When men cheat, women feel heartbreak – not jealousy.
Like the romantic emotions of love and infatuation, the cheating emotions of the two genders differ as much as their genitalia. Although both genders feel a negative emotion when a partner cheats, men feel jealousy and women feel heartbreak.

Jealousy and heartbreak evolved for different purposes.
Jealousy helps men avoid raising another man's child – the worst case scenario for a man's genes. Jealousy does this by coercing men to punish their women for flirting or cheating with other men.

Heartbreak helps women avoid raising a child without a father – the worst case scenario for a woman's genes. Heartbreak does this by punishing women if they become infatuated with men who fall in love with another woman.

While sex causes jealousy, love causes heartbreak.
Women do not feel heartbreak when men have sex with another woman. They feel heartbreak when men fall in love with another woman. Women don't, for example, feel heartbreak when their man pays for sex with a prostitute. Women do feel heartbreak when their man pays for presents that he gives to another woman.

This gender difference can be seen in the questions people ask when they learn their partner has cheated. While men want to know what type of sex that the other man enjoyed, women want to know how much money was spent on the other woman.

20

While jealousy can be stopped, heartbreak cannot.
Men can stop feeling jealousy if they punish their woman. Women cannot stop heartbreak by punishing their man. They will always feel heartbreak when they think about their man cheating – even if they get mad at him.

Jealousy has a stop because it encourages men to act now – before it's too late to prevent intercourse with another man. It gets men to act now by delivering a strong negative effect that can be stopped by acting. The sooner a man punishes his woman, the sooner he stops feeling the stabbing pain of jealousy.

Heartbreak doesn't have a stop because it doesn't encourage women to act now. There's no point in getting a woman to act now because it's too late if a man has fallen in love with another woman – that can't be undone or prevented. Instead, it teaches women to avoid lotharios – men who pretend to be in love to get sex – by giving women a painful reminder when they see similar men in the future.

If publicly embarrassed by a cheating man, a woman may also feel revenge.
Revenge is a negative emotion we all feel when we're harmed by rule breaking – see Chapter 12. Cheating by itself doesn't make people feel revenge. While cheating breaks the rules of relationship exclusivity, it doesn't cause real harm. The cheater has fun, but the cheated on person is not harmed – unless there is public embarrassment.

If a woman if publicly embarrassed by a man's cheating, she will feel humiliation – see Chapter 9. That harm will then cause her to feel revenge. And like jealousy, revenge is stopped by harming the offending party. So a publicly embarrassed woman can stop part of her emotional pain by harming her cheating man. However, the pain of heartbreak will remain.

The older a relationship is, the stronger heartbreak feels.
A woman in a one month relationship feels weak heartbreak if her man cheats. A woman in a seven month relationship feels much stronger heartbreak if her man cheats.

<u>Women can only be heartbroken by men they are infatuated with.</u>

If a woman has been in a relationship for more than 8 months, she won't feel heartbreak if her man cheats.

If a woman has been in a relationship for less than 8 months and her man cheats, she will feel heartbreak. And she will always feel heartbreak when she thinks of him cheating – even after she stops being infatuated with him. Men permanently harm relationships when they cheat – not just by eroding trust, but also because they scar women by forever making them feel heartbreak.

<u>Women are more cautious after feeling heartbreak.</u>

Women who haven't felt heartbreak are less cautious about relationships. They've yet to feel how painful heartbreak can be. Woman who've felt heartbreak are more skeptical of men. They've learned the hard way to avoid lotharios.

Chapter 6
Affection

You feel affection when you see or hear familiar people.
And the longer you've known someone, the stronger the affection they make you feel when you see or hear them. You typically feel the strongest affection when you see or hear your family – you've typically known them the longest.

If you don't get enough affection, you feel loneliness.
Affection and loneliness operate like eating and hunger. If you don't eat enough, you feel hunger. If you don't get enough affection, you feel loneliness. Most people don't get enough affection to avoid loneliness.

You only get strong affection from intimate interaction.
The strength of affection you feel from any particular person is primarily determined by how long you've known them. It's also affected by how intimate your interaction is – the more intimate, the stronger the affection. You feel weak affection if you just see a familiar person in the distance. You feel much stronger affection when you are with a familiar person and make eye contact, see them smile or hear them talk.

You can't get affection from texting, emails or social networking.
You only feel affection when you see or hear somebody. A text, email, or posting is just typed communication from somebody, not their image or voice.

It's easy to think you're getting affection when you're social networking. You're intensively and frequently interacting with many people. However, you're not getting what counts – the sight or sound of somebody.

You can also get affection from alternatives to real people.

Recorded or transmitted people make you feel affection. You feel affection, for example, when you watch videos of family members or your favorite sitcom. You also feel affection when you hear a voice mail from an old friend or a popular personality on the radio.

Pets make you feel affection. Pets make us feel affection because they spend a lot of time with us and have features that are similar to humans. We both have stereoscopic vision and routinely make eye contact with each other. Like humans, the longer you've known a pet, the stronger the affection they make you feel.

Music makes you feel affection. And the more familiar the music, the stronger the affection you feel. You can always count on an oldie to make you happy. Music with vocals makes you feel stronger affection than purely instrumental music. And you feel stronger affection when you dance or sing along to music.

You can get most, but not enough affection from alternatives to real people.
Getting affection from real people requires work. You have to coordinate when and where you'll meet the other person. And the other person might be late or not show. In addition, real people can also make you feel negative emotions like revenge, envy or humiliation.

Getting affection from alternatives to real people is much easier. You don't have to coordinate a meeting. You just watch TV or walk your dog when and where you want to. And there's no risk you'll feel negative emotions like envy. Pet numbers keep growing because they're easier than real people.

Unfortunately, alternatives alone cannot provide enough affection to avoid loneliness. The affection you get from alternatives is weaker than the affection you get from real people. If you only got your affection from alternatives, you'd be lonely. You have to get at least some of your affection from real people to avoid loneliness.

Replace lost sources of affection.
Over time, you'll lose sources of affection – permanently and temporarily. You permanently lose sources of affection, for example, when you end a romantic relationship or retire from a full-time job. You temporarily lose multiple sources of affection, for example, when you take an overnight business trip.

By actively replacing these sources, you can avoid becoming lonely. If you lose a romantic partner, for example, find a new partner. If you retire from full-time work, start volunteering. If you take an overnight business trip, use Skype to interact with family.

Sources of affection should be viewed as similar to sources of food. If your regular supermarket closed, you'd find another one to avoid becoming hungry. If you lose a regular source of affection, find another to avoid becoming lonely.

Affection is the emotion that remains when romance ends.
After men stop feeling monogynic love and women stop feeling infatuation, the weaker positive emotion they continue to feel from each other is affection. It's mistakenly believed to be a weaker form of love. It's not.

In addition to being weaker, affection motivates people differently than love or infatuation. Monogynic love rewards men for making a woman happy. Infatuation rewards women for being sexually stimulating to men. Affection just rewards people for being with others – whether they're happy or not. Affection doesn't motivate people to please others – like love and infatuation.

Another difference is duration. Love and infatuation have limited durations, but affection does not. You'll stop feeling love or infatuation for somebody, but you'll always feel affection for them. And it only grows stronger with time.

Affection is important to deciding whether to continue a relationship.
Once love and infatuation end, romantic partners question whether to continue their relationship. If they stay together, they'll be settling for the moderately strong emotion of affection.

If they split and find a new partner, they'll again feel the fireworks of monogynic love or infatuation. But those fireworks will end – as they did before. And then they are just left with affection again. But that affection will not be as strong as the affection they would be feeling had they stayed with their previous partner.

When people are younger, they enjoy riding the roller-coaster of many romantic partners. As people get older, the romantic emotions are easier to resist and affection becomes a more important source of happiness. So people usually switch mid-life from riding the romantic roller coaster to growing affection with one partner.

Deciding when to leave the romantic roller coaster and focus on growing affection with one partner is an important life decision. The later you switch, the more you enjoy the romantic emotions early in life. The earlier you switch, the stronger the affection you enjoy later in life.

Later in life, affection becomes the primary source of happiness.
In the first half of your life, happiness is dominated by three positive emotions: love/infatuation, pride and affection. In the second half of your life, love/infatuation and pride become less important – leaving affection as your most important source of happiness.

Key to feeling strong affection later in life are long-term sources of affection.
The strength of affection you feel later in life is primarily determined by how familiar your sources are. Ideally, your sources would be long-term – people you've known for many decades. Those sources will make you feel the strongest affection.

To ensure that you have long-term sources of affection later in life, earlier in life you must accumulate the decades of time interacting with those people who will become your long-term sources of affection.

Siblings are better long-term sources of affection than parents or children.
Siblings will be with you longer than parents or children. Parents will die before you. Children will be there when you die, but were not there when you were young – like siblings were.

Old friends are better long-term sources of affection than siblings.
First, old friends can make you feel affection as strong as siblings. The difference in the strength of affection you feel from someone you've known for 25 years is not noticeably different than someone you've known for 40 years.

Second, you or your friends are less likely to envy each other. Envy is a negative emotion you feel when a peer does better than you – see Chapter 10. The more similar a peer is, the stronger the envy you feel. And your siblings are your most similar peers. Even slight differences in rank among siblings makes somebody feel envy. Much less so with friends. People seek out people of similar rank to avoid this problem – they don't want to feel envy.

Third, friends try harder than siblings. Siblings believe siblings love each other. So they assume that you'll always come back – even if they treat you poorly. Friends don't assume you love them. They assume you'll stop being friends if they treat you poorly. So they try harder than siblings to be polite, punctual or interesting.

Choosing friends as long-term sources of affection requires making a friends a higher priority than family and siblings in particular. This will make you unpopular in the short term, but happier in the long term. You'll feel strong affection from people who work harder at friendship.

Making others feel affection is the easiest way to be popular.
When socializing, there are three positive emotions you can make others feel: pride, humor or affection. Compliments make others feel pride. Jokes or gossip makes others feel humor. Interacting with others in any way makes them feel affection.

It's difficult to make others feel pride or humor on an ongoing basis. People only feel pride when you elevate their rank. And it's not possible to elevate someone's rank indefinitely. Jokes or gossip only make someone feel humor the first time you tell them a joke or gossip. And it's not possible to have infinite supply of new jokes or gossip.

By comparison, it's easy to make others feel affection on an ongoing basis. You only have to interact – no insightful compliment or witty jokes required. Just asking questions about them does the job. And the more you interact with them, the stronger the affection they feel.

Popular people are good at making others feel affection.
They spend a lot of time interacting with others. And they specifically make it a habit to <u>smile</u> and make <u>eye-contact</u> while <u>talking</u> to others – three of the best ways to make others feel affection.

Affection makes a difference to your physical health.
In multiple studies and historical situations, the amount of affection that people feel has made a significant difference to their physical health. These studies and historical accounts do not refer to affection explicitly – instead, they refer to how many family and friends somebody interacts with.

For example, longevity studies show that the people that live the longest are those with the largest number of family and friends. And the people who recover from illness the fastest are those that have the most visits from family and friends.

The people most likely to survive the winter in the Donner party or among the Mayflower pilgrims were the people who travelled with family, not those who travelled alone.

Affection evolved to encourage you to be with others so you can learn by observing them or they can learn by observing you. If you're not with others, which would be the case if you have no family or friends, then you're not helping to transfer learning. So it makes biological sense that people who feel less affection would die sooner. They're not helping to transfer learning.

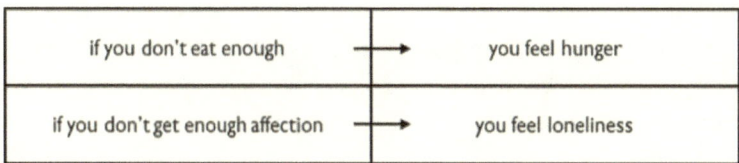

if you don't eat enough	→	you feel hunger
if you don't get enough affection	→	you feel loneliness

You feel loneliness when you don't get enough affection.
Loneliness works like hunger. If you don't eat enough, you start feeling hunger. And the longer it's been since you've eaten, the stronger hunger becomes. Similarly, if you don't get enough affection, you start feeling loneliness. And the longer it's been since you've felt affection, the stronger loneliness becomes.

Proof that loneliness is caused by the absence of affection – meaning interaction with <u>familiar</u> people – can be found in any large city. Despite being surrounded by thousands of people, many city dwellers are lonely. They're interacting with many people, but not with familiar people.

A possible synonym for loneliness is sadness.

Loneliness makes you cry.
Crying here means tears running down your face, not wailing or other vocalizations. When you become lonely, you will cry – unless you suppress it.

Crying is often suppressed.
The urge to cry can be suppressed, like the urge to sneeze can be suppressed. Crying is suppressed because it suggests emotional instability.

The behaviors that suppress crying are subtle, but can be detected when people release suppressed crying. When they begin crying, their breathing is labored and their chins tremble. Their breathing is labored because tensing your diaphragm suppresses crying. Their chins tremble because tensing your facial muscles suppresses crying.

Suppressed crying is released by any strong emotion.
People are unable to suppress crying when they are mentally distracted by a strong emotion. People release suppressed crying when they feel negative emotions like humiliation. And they do it when they feel positive emotions like pride or affection – which explains happy crying. Oscar winners cry during acceptance speeches because they feel strong pride. People meeting loved ones at the airport cry because they feel strong affection.

Contagious crying is the release of suppressed crying. Seeing somebody cry makes you feel the negative emotion of compassion which then causes you to release suppressed crying.

Only loneliness makes you cry.
The release of suppressed crying by any strong emotion makes it seem like any emotion can make you cry. However, there is only one root cause for crying – loneliness. If you cry, you're lonely – it doesn't matter what emotion you're feeling when you cry. And if you're not lonely, you won't cry – even if you feel a strong emotion.

You can use crying to learn how much affection you need.
It's hard to know if you're getting enough affection to avoid loneliness. Affection is hard to mentally separate from other positive emotions. Even if you could mentally separate it, it's hard to know if you getting strong enough affection to avoid loneliness.

Because crying is only caused by loneliness, it's a reliable indicator that you need more affection.

If you cry once a week or more, you are lonely.
Keep increasing how much affection you get each week until you cry less than once a week. At that point, you'll stop feeling loneliness and be happier. It'll be hard to pin down why you're happier because the happiness is not tied to a single event or thought. You'll just be in a generally good mood every day – because you stopped feeling loneliness.

Most people are lonely.
Prior to the industrial revolution, we spent virtually all of our lives with our families and friends – our most important sources of affection. Now we spend the majority of our waking hours at work with people we've known for minutes or months, not years or decades.

Crying is the best evidence that most people are lonely. Most people cry in tear jerker movies or other situations that cause strong emotions. They wouldn't be crying if they weren't lonely.

With a little affection planning, it's easy to avoid loneliness.
You plan your eating to avoid becoming hungry. You plan, for example, when and where you'll eat. You get enough money and food to ensure you have full meals. You should plan getting affection the same way.

You should plan to interact with enough people and enough hours to ensure you're not lonely. And you should think about how you'll interact with those people to ensure you're getting strong affection when you're together. Are you, for example, watching a movie or having dinner facing each other?

Chapter 8
Pride

	your rank	another's rank	
pride	⬆	⬆	envy
humiliation	⬇	⬇	humor

Pride is one of the four rank emotions.

The rank emotions have a profound and pervasive effect on everyone's happiness and behavior. They're the main reason we compete and the main reason we cooperate.

You feel pride when your rank rises.

You feel pride, for example, when you:

- graduate from school
- win an award or contest
- are the underdog and win
- are complimented by others
- get a job, get promoted or get a raise
- get better assets, such as cars or clothes
- are treated like an equal by a higher-ranking person

Synonyms for pride include elation and jubilation.

The bigger your rise in rank, the stronger pride feels.

Graduating from college, for example, makes you feel stronger pride than just passing a course. Getting a 20% raise at work makes you feel stronger pride than just getting a 10% raise.

When successful people describe their life stories, they usually start by emphasizing their impoverished beginning. They do this to maximize their rise in rank – which then maximizes the strength of the pride they feel.

Pride is caused by higher rank, not high rank.

Rookies feel pride, but veteran all-stars don't. Rookies are low rank, but higher than before. Veteran all-stars are high rank, but not higher rank.

Recent nursing graduates feel pride, but established doctors don't. Recent nursing graduates are low rank, but higher than before. Established doctors are high rank, but not higher rank.

Pride rewards those who improve – even those at the bottom. And pride does not reward those who do not improve – even those at the top.

Strong pride makes you smile involuntarily.

Winners beam after winning. And they often try to hide their smiling. They're uncomfortable with their involuntary reaction. And they want to avoid making others feel envy.

You feel pride in three different situations:
- when others recognize your higher rank
- when you seek recognition from others of your higher rank
- when you alone recognize your higher rank

You feel the strongest pride when others recognize your higher rank.

This happens when you graduate from school, win an award, are complimented or get a promotion.

Being recognized by others makes you feel strongest pride because it's most authentic. You feel pride when you conclude that your rank has increased. And your rank is assigned to you by others. So the only way to confidently conclude that your rank has increased is when others voluntarily assign you a higher rank.

You feel weak pride when you seek recognition from others.

This happens when you show others your achievements, assets or connections.

Seeking recognition from others forces others to recognize your higher rank or they seem rude. Consequently, you can't confidently conclude that they think you're higher rank. The pride you feel is weakened by this uncertainty.

Seeking recognition from others, or bragging, annoys others. They don't enjoy being forced to recognize your achievements or assets so that you can feel pride. It doesn't make them pride. If they're former peers, it makes them feel envy – see Chapter 10.

Braggarts rationalize bragging by telling themselves that others share their pride. However, few people share someone's pride. The only people are those directly involved in somebody's accomplishment such as parents, coaches, teachers or mentors.

You feel weak pride when you alone recognize your higher rank.
This happens, for example, when you run a faster time while jogging or the first time you accomplish a difficult task without errors.

This version of pride is what is meant by a sense of accomplishment. It's weak because you're the only one concluding that your rank has increased.

You feel imaginary pride more often than real pride.
You feel imaginary pride when you imagine your rank increasing in the future. We all do this when working towards a long term goal, such as getting a college degree or buying a house. To keep yourself motivated while you study for exams or work overtime for extra income, you imagine how you'll feel when you reach your goal. That interim reward is imaginary pride.

Imaginary pride is not as strong as real pride. You feel weak pride when you imagine yourself being handed a diploma at a graduation ceremony. You feel much stronger pride when it actually happens.

People buy lottery tickets to enjoy imaginary pride. It doesn't make sense to buy lottery tickets based on the odds alone. The expected value of winning is less than the ticket price. However, it does make sense if you include the ticket holder's enjoyment of imaginary pride. A ticket holder can credibly tell themselves that they could be a winner. They can feel imaginary pride that non-ticket holders cannot.

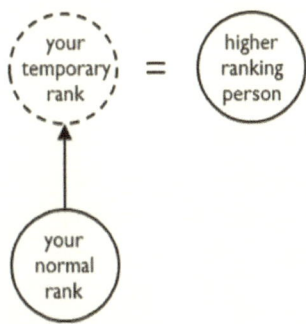

You feel pride when a higher-ranking person treats you like an equal.
If a higher-ranking person treats you like an equal, it feels like your rank has risen to their higher level. This happens when you meet a famous person. Feeling your rank rise to the level of the famous person makes you feel pride.

Famous people know they have this effect on ordinary people. They know that spending a few minutes being down-to-earth with ordinary people leaves them with a strong positive memory. Afterwards, those ordinary people tell their friends and family how likeable the famous person was. It wasn't the famous person they liked. It was the pride the famous person made them feel.

A peculiar example of this occurs when bystanders are interviewed by news reporters at the scene of tragedies. These people often smile when interviewed despite describing the grim details of the tragedy. They smile involuntarily because they feel pride – they're on television, they're famous.

Pride is temporary.
You only feel pride while your higher rank is new to you. Once your rank is no longer new to you, you stop feeling pride. A new car or a promotion, for example, will only make you feel pride for about a year.

As you'll read ahead, many people mistakenly assume that pride is permanent. This mistaken assumption leads to bad decision making, particularly regarding careers and shopping.

Not realizing that pride is temporary leads to career mistakes.
Most people choose a career based on how they imagine they'll feel if they worked in that field. A college student, for example, will decide whether to become a doctor based on how he imagines he'll feel being a doctor. He imagines himself in a white lab coat with patients and nurses looking to him for answers. And he imagines the reaction of his family and friends when he announces that he's a doctor. These images make him feel imaginary pride.

This approach is flawed because it assumes that pride is permanent. Prospective doctors, for example, assume they'll always feel that pride they imagine feeling when patients look to them or family learns they're a doctor.

In reality, the pride that people imagine feeling is temporary. A doctor, for example, will only feel pride for a few years at most. Once he becomes accustomed to his rank of doctor, he'll stop feeling pride. He's then left with the daily grind of the job. For many doctors, who enjoy intellectual challenges, the daily grind of interacting with patients is tortuously boring. This bad outcome occurs in many white collar jobs – doctors, dentists, lawyers, accountants and pilots.

Instead of imaging day 1 at work, career choices should be made by imagining day 1000. Instead of focusing on the reaction of family or friends, a career decision should focus on the required day-to-day activities. Prospective doctors, for example, should focus on whether they want to spend their days closely interacting with sick people. Prospective lawyers should focus on whether they want to spend their days scrutinizing detail in old cases or contracts.

Not realizing that pride is temporary leads to shopping mistakes.
Most people decide to buy a product based on how they imagine they'll feel when they own it. For products that signal higher rank, like expensive cars and clothes, they primarily imagine feeling pride.

This approach is flawed because it assumes that pride is permanent. Prospective buyers assume they'll always feel that pride they imagine feeling when others see them driving a new car or wearing new shoes.

In reality, they won't enjoy that pride for more than a year at most. Once the pride is gone, they'll be left with a credit card bill and a product that doesn't make them happy.

A better way to evaluate a purchase is to ask yourself if you'd still buy it if nobody else saw it. If you still want to buy a car or shoes in this scenario, then you're not buying because of pride. It's hard to imagine nobody seeing a product. So you may need to be creative with your questions. For example, would you still buy an article of designer clothing if the designer's tags were removed after you buy it?

Pride motivates people to start, but not continue self-improvement.
While you're losing weight, for example, your rank is increasing and you're feeling pride. That pride is the motivation that keeps you dieting or exercising. It offsets the hunger of dieting or the pain of exercising.

Eventually your weight reaches a floor, which means your rank reaches a plateau and you stop feeling pride. Without the offset of pride, you're no longer willing to keep dieting or exercising. You go back to eating too much or not exercising enough.

Dieting or self-improvement would be better achieved by not using pride. Instead of focusing on weight loss or running times, focus on what can be done without the need for pride. Instead of thinking about how fast you ran, for example, see how far you can run without feeling pain. If it's painful, you won't do it when the pride is gone. If it's pleasant, you'll happily add it to your daily routine – without the need for pride.

Also, don't tell others how much you're improving – it'll encourage you to seek pride. You should treat exercise like brushing your teeth. You brush your teeth because it's good for your health, not because it makes you feel pride. As a result, you don't tell people about how much cleaner your teeth are.

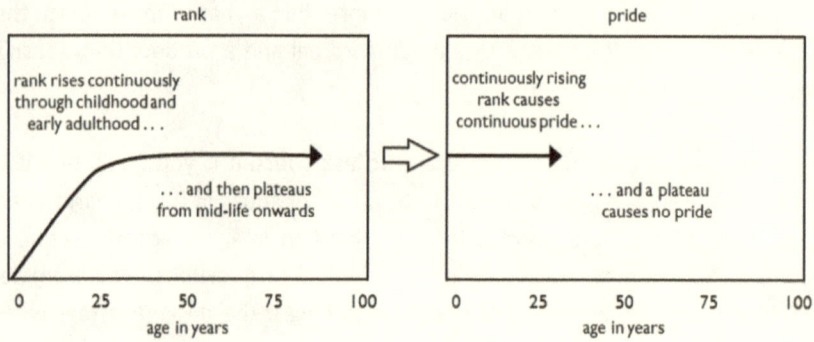

Mid-life crises occur because rank plateaus and pride stops.

Throughout childhood and early adulthood, you experience continuous increases in rank. You keep getting taller. You graduate to another grade each year. You get more and more responsibilities and freedoms. You get a job. You get promoted. You get raises. You get your own place. You buy new assets. This continuous increase in rank produces a continuous feeling of pride.

At mid-life, your rank hits a plateau. You do not grow taller. There are no annual graduations. You've held the same position at work for years. And there is no immediate prospect of promotion. Because your rank has hit a plateau, you no longer feel the continuous feeling of pride you felt for the first 2-3 decades of life.

People in a mid-life crisis make changes to feel pride again. They often try to be younger, which is when they felt more pride. Men buy sports cars. Women get cosmetic surgery. These changes do make people feel pride, but not for long. They'd be happier if they pursued goals that offer the potential to enjoy ongoing pride such as a new career or hobby.

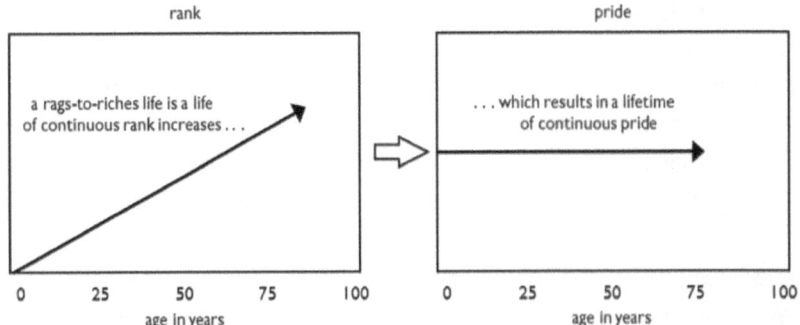

The best life plan is rags-to-riches.

A rags-to-riches life is the story of someone rising from the bottom to the top – meaning a continuous rise in rank. If someone's rank is continually rising throughout their lives, they are continually feeling pride throughout their lives. This life plan maximizes the amount of pride you can feel during a lifetime.

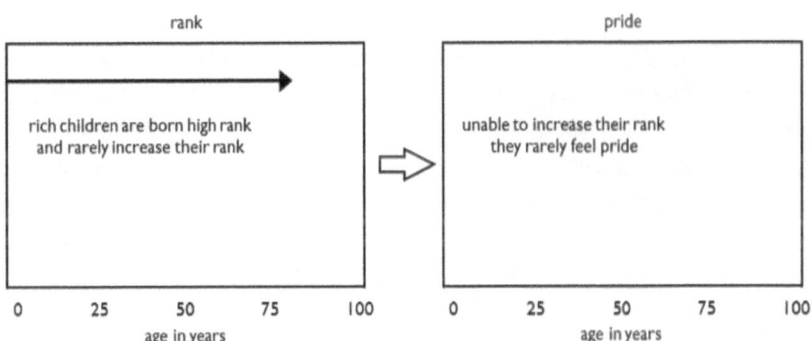

Rich children feel less pride.

Rich children are born high rank and rarely increase their rank – at least in the way that brought their family success. Because they can't increase their rank as easily as others, they don't feel pride as much as others. They find it easier to increase their rank in ways unrelated to the family's success. Consequently, they are often viewed as rebellious or dysfunctional.

Complimenting others is a smart habit.
It costs nothing to compliment someone and it makes them feel pride. Making the people around your feel pride will benefit every aspect of your life – you will get promoted sooner, get a better spouse, have more friends and better adjusted children. Habitually complimenting others is the equivalent to casting sunlight on the garden of people around you – it will bloom more.

Complimenting has to change to keep working.
If you keep paying somebody the same compliment, they will not keep feeling pride. They'll only feel pride the first few times you tell them they are smart or attractive. Once they become accustomed to you telling them they're smart or attractive, they'll stop feeling pride. Repeating the same compliment will just make you annoying.

To keep making someone feel pride, you have to compliment something different each time – different skills, different qualities, different achievements or different assets. It's okay, for example, to keep complimenting somebody about their clothing as long as it's a different article each time.

Pride's temporary nature is why money can't buy happiness.
Money can buy happiness, but only temporarily. If you win the lottery, for example, you'll feel pride when you buy a larger house or fancier car. However, that pride will stop within a couple of years. You may still have the money and assets at that point, but you won't be able to increase your rank further and feel more pride. After feeling very strong pride from winning the lottery, its absence will seem like depression.

Pride's temporary nature explains why rich nations are not happier.
Surveys of national happiness usually show that rich, developed nations are not happier than poorer, less developed nations. That's because pride is the primary emotion people think about when surveyed about their happiness. And a nation feels pride by getting richer, not by being rich. So poor, growing countries feel pride. And rich, non-growing countries do not. National happiness is most correlated with GDP per capita growth, not GDP per capita.

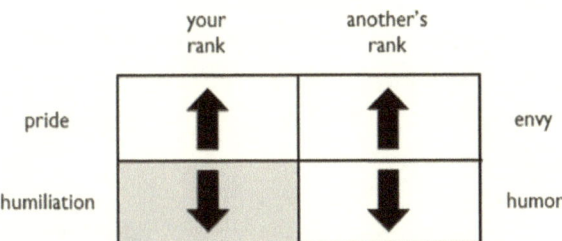

You feel humiliation when your rank falls.

You feel humiliation, for example, when you:

- are the favorite and lose
- are criticized or putdown
- fail to graduate from school
- ask for help with directions or finances
- say sorry, apologize, or admit you were wrong
- are fired, demoted, laid-off or retire from work
- are treated like an equal by a lower-ranking person
- are asked for something without hearing please or thank-you

Synonyms for pride include embarrassment, shame and dejection.

The bigger your fall in rank, the stronger humiliation feels.

Being fired from work, for example, makes you feel stronger humiliation than just getting a bad performance review. Failing a school year makes you feel stronger humiliation than just failing a test.

Humiliation is caused by lower rank, not low rank.

The only criminals who feel humiliation are first-time offenders. Repeat offenders are low rank, but their rank doesn't fall when they reoffend.

Every CEO feels humiliation when they retire. CEO's are high rank, but their rank falls when they retire.

You feel imaginary humiliation more often than real humiliation.

You feel imaginary humiliation when you imagine your rank falling. We all do this when we worry about things that could go wrong – like being laid off or failing a course. We specifically worry about the humiliation we imagine feeling when we tell others – like telling your family you've been laid off or telling your classmates that you failed a course.

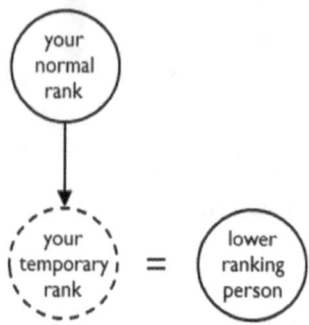

You feel humiliation when a lower-ranking person treats you like an equal.

If a lower-ranking person treats you like an equal, it feels like your rank has fallen to their level. Adults feel humiliation, for example, when a child addresses them by their first name. The Queen feels humiliation if her subjects do not curtsey or bow for her.

People feel vicarious humiliation the first time they use a personal servant.

People are uncomfortable the first time they have a pedicure or hire a maid. They imagine being the lower rank of pedicurist or maid – which makes them feel humiliation.

Pedicurists and maids don't feel humiliation – their rank hasn't fallen. They may have been providing pedicures or cleaning toilets for years. So their rank may be low, but it's not lower.

Humiliation is temporary.

You only feel humiliation while your lower rank is new to you. Once your rank is no longer new to you, you stop feeling humiliation. People who have been fired, for example, stop feeling humiliation after about a year.

Not realizing that humiliation is temporary can lead to big mistakes.
Many people going through a downfall, like being fired, assume the negative emotion they feel is permanent. Unable to face a future of permanent depression, they take drastic steps to avoid it – like becoming addicted to a substance or committing suicide.

The negative emotion they feel is humiliation and it's temporary. It stops when they become accustomed to their new, lower rank. And once the humiliation stops, they're as happy as they were before the downfall – assuming they don't become addicted to a substance or commit suicide.

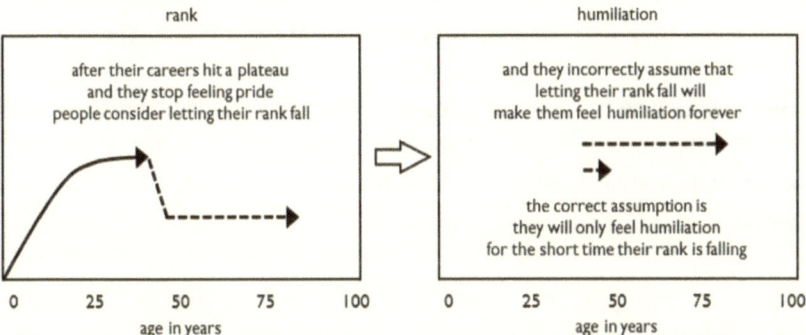

After a mid-life crisis, avoiding humiliation becomes the primary motivation.
At mid-life, most people's rank hits a plateau. Their education, incomes, assets and title do not change significantly from one year to the next. Because their rank has stopped rising, they no longer feel pride. After feeling continuous pride for decades, its absence feels like depression.

At this point, people consider letting their rank fall. Without the reward of pride, people are less willingly to tolerate long hours of work or commuting.

They don't let it fall because of humiliation. They contemplate a career that's less demanding but also less rewarding financially and lower stature. They imagine moving to a smaller house or wearing cheaper clothes. When people imagine that lower rank scenario, they imagine feeling humiliation and they do not like it.

So they decide to not make any changes. They continue in the same career, same hours and same commute. However, their mindset has changed. Instead of working to feel pride, now they work to avoid humiliation. It's a miserable existence that seems unavoidable.

Many of these people give up on finding happiness during the week and live for the weekends instead. Others start eating too much as they try to offset lost pride with food. Others become functional alcoholics – they drink enough to make it through the boredom of the workday, but not enough to prevent them doing the job they've done for years.

People at this juncture in life make a critical assumption about the humiliation they'll feel if they stop working so hard and let their rank fall. They correctly assume they'll feel humiliation, but they incorrectly assume they'll feel it forever. They won't. They'll only feel humiliation for the short time their rank is falling. After the humiliation stops, they'll end up just as happy about work, but working far less – leaving more time for hobbies or family – new sources of happiness.

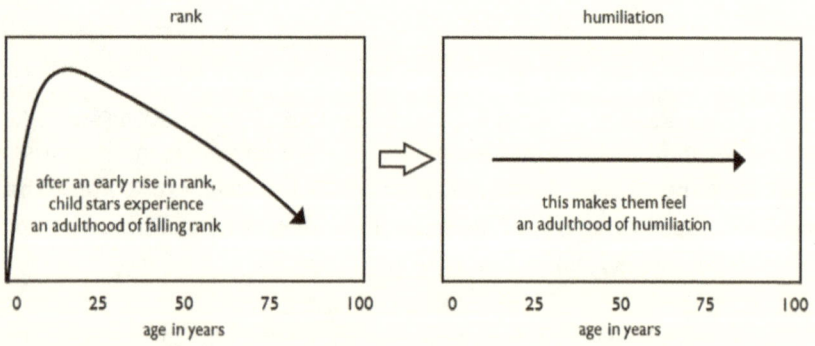

Child stars have the worst life plan.
During childhood, child stars feel strong pride as their rank rockets to stardom. However, that's usually followed by an adulthood of falling rank which makes them feel an adulthood of humiliation – which they often try to mask with drugs or alcohol.

This problem affects anybody who enjoys a temporary spike in rank – like Olympic gold medalists in purely amateur sports. Their rapid rise in rank makes them feel a surge of happiness that ends after a year or two. After feeling that extreme happiness, they then experience continual humiliation while their rank continually falls back to average.

Asking for help makes people feel humiliation.

People are reluctant to ask for help because it lowers their rank and makes them feel humiliation. Men are reluctant to ask for directions, for example, because it lowers their rank to non-navigator. They would rather use trial-and-error to find their destination than feel the humiliation of asking for help. Adults don't like asking others for financial help, for example, because it lowers their rank below independent adult. Many would rather be homeless than feel the humiliation of asking for help.

Saying sorry or apologizing makes people feel humiliation.

People are reluctant to apologize because it lowers their rank and makes them feel humiliation. If you apologize for being late, for example, you are stating that your rank has fallen to that of somebody who is inconsiderate.

The strong reluctance of people to say sorry or apologize is proof that humiliation is painful. Apologizing is an easy way to stop another person feeling revenge towards you. Three little words gets rid of an enemy. Despite this, people don't apologize because they don't want to feel the pain of humiliation.

You feel humiliation when others don't say please or thank-you.

Saying please and thank-you is a promise of reciprocity. Saying "please pass the salt", for example, is equivalent to saying "if you pass the salt, I'll return the favor if you ask me". Saying "thank you" is equivalent to saying "I confirm that I'll return the favor".

If someone doesn't say please and thank-you, they expect you to cooperate without the promise of reciprocity. This implies that you're their servant – which lowers your rank and makes you feel humiliation.

We say please and thank-you to actual servants to mask the fact that they're lower rank. Customers and bosses, for example, say please and thank-you to waitresses or employees to avoid making them feel humiliation. Instead, they hope to make them feel pride by treating them like equals.

People fail to fully mature because humiliation stops them hearing feedback.
People need feedback from others to fully mature. They need to know, for example, when they are hurtful to others so they know what to change. Otherwise their hurtful personality traits will persist and their development will be frozen.

Unfortunately, getting feedback from others makes people feel humiliation. As a result, they become defensive and disagree with the feedback before considering it. And the person giving the feedback is less inclined to give feedback in the future.

The solution is to develop the habit of just listening when others give feedback. You can't stop feeling humiliation. However, you can anticipate it and choose to listen instead of being defensive. People that develop the habit of just listening to feedback are more mature and more likeable.

Actively using humiliation can help maintain self-improvement.
People commonly use pride to motivate themselves to improve. However, pride is good for starting, but not for maintaining self-improvement. People feel pride when they start losing weight, for example, which offsets the hunger of dieting or pain of exercising. But their pride stops when their weight reaches a floor. Without pride to motivate them, most people fall back to their old ways.

Actively using humiliation would help maintain improvement when pride stops. People who want to maintain their weight, for example, could force themselves to attend pool parties or take beach vacations. Or they could put full-length mirrors in their bathrooms or bedrooms. The parties and mirrors will force them to feel humiliation if they become overweight. The threat of humiliation will prevent them from regaining weight – in the same way that the threat of humiliation motivates people to soldier on after a mid-life crisis.

You blush when you feel pride quickly followed by humiliation.
You will blush, for example, if you walk into a room of people who look at you and then laugh at a big stain on your crotch. You felt pride when you first walked in the room because everybody was looking at you. You then felt humiliation when you realized that you had a stain on your crotch.

Blushing makes others feel compassion instead of humor. At first, the people in the room would feel humor when they saw your stained crotch. They would then feel compassion when they saw you blushing.

Blushing evolved to encourage learning by trial-and-error. It blunts the pain of humiliation that occurs during errors by encouraging others to help instead of laughing. If errors don't hurt as much, people are more willing undertake the trials.

Insecure people are overly sensitive to humiliation.
Insecure people are overly concerned with avoiding a fall in rank because it makes them feel humiliation. They're frequently checking their appearance, for example, for anything out of place. Or they frequently ask friends if their appearance or behavior is embarrassing. Avoiding humiliation becomes their primary concern when socializing.

The highest ranked people are more concerned with humiliation than pride.
The people at the top are more likely to feel humiliation than others – they have nowhere to go but down. And they could feel much stronger humiliation than others – they have farther to fall than anyone else.

" The desire of acquiring the comforts of the world
haunts the imagination of the poor,
and the dread of losing them that of the rich."

Alexis de Tocqueville

You feel envy when the rank of a former peer rises above yours.
You feel envy, for example, when:
- a neighbor gets a better car than you
- a co-worker gets promoted before you
- a teammate gets an award and you don't
- a sibling gets more attention from your parents
- a college classmate gets a better paying job than you
- a high school classmate goes to a better college than you

Envy and jealousy are different emotions – see the end of this chapter.

You only envy former peers.
You envy, for example, a classmate who does better than you, but not a student that was just one year behind or ahead of you. You envy a sibling that has a better car than you, but not a stranger that has the same car.

Only former peers make you feel envy because they were on an equal footing with you at some point. If they were on an equal footing, they had the same potential as you. If they did better than you, then you did not reach your full potential. Envy evolved to coerce to reach your full potential.

The more similar a former peer was, the stronger envy feels.
You might expect the strength of envy to be tied to changes in rank – like pride and humiliation. Pride is stronger for bigger rises in rank. And humiliation is stronger for bigger falls in rank.

Similarly, you might expect envy to be stronger for bigger rises in a former peer's rank. A sibling with a house five times the size of your house would make you feel stronger envy that a sibling with a house only twice the size of yours. However, this is not the case. Both siblings would make you feel the same envy.

Instead of changes in rank, the strength of envy is tied to peer similarity. The more a former peer had in common with you, the stronger the envy you feel. Siblings make you feel stronger envy than classmates. Twins make each other feel stronger envy than regular siblings. The strength of envy is tied to peer similarity to focus you on those people whose potential most matches yours.

Unlike the other rank emotions, envy is permanent.

The other rank emotions stop without any effort on your part. Pride stops when your higher rank is not higher anymore. Humiliation stops when your lower rank is not lower anymore. Humor stops the second time you hear a joke. Envy does not stop. You feel it forever – unless you close the gap with your former peer. In effect, envy coerces you to close the gap.

Envy causes of a lot of unhappiness.

Envy affects many people for many years. While pride affects the one person whose rank has increased, envy affects everybody the higher-ranked person was a peer with – their siblings, their classmates, their teammates, their neighbors, their co-workers. While the higher-ranked person only feels pride for a year or two, all of those former peers feel envy forever. And it gets worse.

The siblings and former classmates of a higher-ranked person feel the strongest envy. And siblings and former classmates are the people a higher-ranked person is most likely to socialize with for two reasons. First, siblings and former classmates make them feel the strongest affection. Second, they feel more pride when they are with former peers than strangers – former peers know their rank has increased, strangers don't. And it gets still worse.

People are not supposed to feel envy. Because envy is inconvenient for parents and bosses, they deal with it by dismissing it as immature. So in addition to feeling envy, envious people are also led to believe they have a maturity problem.

Envy is a normal adult response.
Envy is not a childish reaction you "should get over". And envy is not some minor emotion that can be suppressed like a sneeze. If you feel envy, you should not feel bad, broken, immature or abnormal. Envy is as normal as pride, humiliation and humor.

Openly acknowledging envy would avoid some unhappiness.
Everyone would be happier if we recognized that envy is as normal as pride. Envious people would stop wondering if they're immature. And high-ranked people would stop wondering why their former peers seem hostile towards them. They would realize that all former peers envy people who outrank them.

Avoid people you envy.
There are three ways to avoid feeling envy. First, you could increase your rank to match your former peer – which is what envy coerces you to do. However, it's usually difficult to match the rank of former peers who have excelled – particularly late in life. Even if you could match one former peer who has excelled, there are always others who have excelled in a different way. You'll never match the rank of every one of your former peers.

Second, you could reduce the rank of former peers – as often happens, unfortunately. Envy of more successful people and peoples has often led to harmful outcomes. This is usually unlawful and more harmful to you. And it does not address the underlying difference that enabled the former peer to excel ahead of you. Whatever propelled them ahead of you will do so again.

Third, you could avoid people you envy. It's much easier than trying to increase your rank or reduce theirs.

You may think you should "be a bigger person" and "get over your envy" so you can socialize with people you envy. However, you won't enjoy yourself. You'll have to smile politely and feel envy while they show you their stuff or talk about their achievements.

So don't try to get over your envy – you can't. Instead, don't socialize with people you envy. Don't socialize, for example, with siblings or classmates that have done better than you. And definitely do not attend any class reunions.

Avoid people that envy you.

If you have become higher-ranked, it's best to avoid former peers. They 'll be envious and envious people tend to be harmful. They can't help it. Even the nicest people want to harm the people they envy. It's better to find new friends of any rank than to continue socializing with your old co-workers or classmates. New friends will not envy you – new friends can't be former peers.

When you can't avoid people that envy you, don't "share your success".

While you may be able to avoid some people that envy you, you can't avoid all of them – in particular, your siblings. You'll tempted to share your success with these people. You'll think that sharing your success also shares your pride with them. It doesn't. Your rank increased. Theirs didn't. Sharing your success just makes them feel envy – regardless of how much they smile and congratulate you. Instead, focus on them. They'll enjoy your attention and be pleasantly surprised they don't feel envy.

Avoid making others envy others.

In a leadership role, it's easy to make others envy others. Parents, bosses, teachers and coaches can cause envy just by complimenting one person. People in these positions assume there's no downside to praising somebody. This assumption only considers what the praised person feels. It doesn't consider the impact of the praise on the peers of the praised person.

Publicly praising somebody makes one person feel pride and many others feel envy. That envy will demotivate others and make them less supportive of the person who received the praise. It's better to praise individuals privately. The individual still feels pride and others don't feel envy.

If you must praise somebody publicly, make sure it's clearly tied to behavior or performance you want from others. If it's clearly tied, then others are more likely to try stopping their envy by replicating the praised behavior. If many others replicate the behavior of the praised person, then it'll be worth causing mass envy.

The best reason to be top-ranked is not feeling envy.

Pride is not the best reason to be top-ranked. After the top-ranked feel pride for a year or two, they worry about feeling humiliation – like everyone else.

Unlike everyone else, the top-ranked do not feel envy. Since they are top-ranked, there is nobody to envy. But everybody below them feels the ongoing stabbing pain of envy towards somebody.

Not feeling envy is one reason the top-ranked should be happier than others. Unfortunately, they don't seem to realize this – they're usually unhappy because they expected to feel pride forever.

jealousy	envy
men feel it when their women make another man feel sexual pleasure	everyone feels it when a former peer achieves higher rank

Jealousy and envy are different emotions.

People incorrectly assume there is one negative emotion you feel when somebody has something you want. And jealousy and envy are both used to refer to this emotion. A jealous man, for example, wants a woman who is with another man. An envious person wants an asset or privilege that somebody else has.

There are two negative emotions with fundamentally different purposes.

This book uses jealousy to refer to the negative emotion that men feel when their woman makes another man feel sexual pleasure. Jealousy evolved to help men avoid raising another man's child.

This book uses envy to refer to the negative emotion that everyone feels when a former peer achieves higher rank. Envy evolved to coerce you to reach your full potential.

Simply put, jealousy is about sex and envy is about rank.

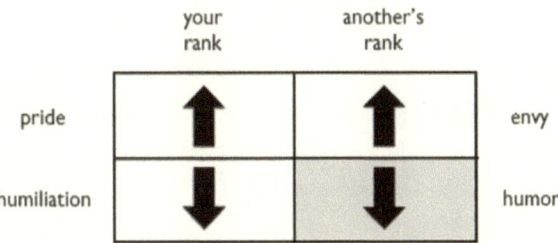

You feel humor when you learn that somebody made a rank-reducing mistake that you could make.

You feel humor, for example, when you:

- hear a joke or see a comedy
- hear a putdown or witness a prank
- hear gossip or read tabloid news
- hear criticism or criticize others
- see a favorite upset

Synonyms for humor include funny and schadenfreude, but not laughter.

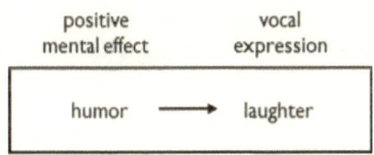

Laughter is different than humor.

Humor is a positive mental effect. Laughter is a vocal expression that usually follows humor.

Laughter is a <u>voluntary</u> expression. People can choose not laugh when they do feel humor – not laughing when something funny occurs at a funeral, for example. And people can choose to laugh when they don't feel humor – laughing at the boss's dumb jokes, for example.

Laughter seems involuntary because it's a deeply ingrained habit, like walking or talking. You don't think about walking or talking – you just do it out of habit. Similarly, you don't think about laughing – you just laugh out of habit when you feel humor.

Because laughter is a voluntary expression, it's an unreliable signal that you or other people feel humor. In fact, most of the humor you feel occurs when you don't laugh – as you'll read ahead.

Humor is far more than jokes or comedy.
You also feel humor when you hear a putdown, hear gossip, criticize others or see a favorite upset. In each of these situations, you are learning about somebody making a rank-reducing mistake. When you hear a putdown, for example, you may hear that somebody is a liar. When you hear gossip, you may hear that somebody was caught cheating. When you criticize somebody, you may learn from yourself that somebody is always late. When you see a favorite upset, you may see a champion defeated by a basement dweller.

Humor evolved to reward you for learning about others making rank-reducing mistakes. So any situation where you learn about others making rank-reducing mistakes makes you feel humor – including gossip, criticism, putdowns and seeing favorites upset.

Gossip is a bigger source of humor than jokes and comedy combined.
On average, people spend a few hours a day in non-work conversations and gossip dominates those conversations. By comparison, they average less than an hour a day listening to jokes or watching comedies.

Criticism – hearing it or giving it – is a surprising source of humor.
Criticizing somebody involves pointing out errors they're making that reduce their rank – and that makes you feel humor whether you are hearing others criticized or giving criticism to others. If you are hearing criticism, you are learning about another's mistakes from the criticizer. If you are giving criticism, you are learning about another's mistakes from yourself.

It's surprising that criticism is a source of humor because it doesn't seem like fun. Nobody's laughing when somebody is criticized.

Nobody's laughing because criticizers need to maintain a humorless exterior while criticizing others. If criticizers showed enjoyment while criticizing others, they'd reveal their real motive for criticizing others – to feel humor. If the person being criticized realized that a criticizer is enjoying humor, they wouldn't bother listening to the criticism. The criticizer is not trying to help them – the criticizer wants to have fun at their expense.

Humor has four requirements.
If comedy, gossip, criticism or jokes do not meet all of the following requirements, they will not make you feel humor:
1. a mistake by another person is described
2. which reduces the other person's rank
3. which you could also make
4. which is news to you

1. You feel humor when you learn about mistakes, but not about misfortune.
You feel humor if you see a man slip on banana. He made the mistake of not looking where he is walking. You don't feel humor if you see a man knocked down by a falling tree branch. He suffered the misfortune of being under the tree at the wrong time. While a mistake makes people feel humor, misfortune makes people feel compassion – see Chapter 14.

It's important to note the subtle difference between mistakes and misfortune. Jokes about mistakes are liked. Jokes about misfortune are disliked – often intensely. Jokes about being a drunkard, for example, are liked, but jokes about being mentally challenged are not.

Being fat is considered a mistake by some and misfortune by others. If your audience believes that weight is not something people can control, jokes about being fat will not be funny.

Being short is not a mistake, but many people make short jokes anyways. Short jokes don't make people feel humor. Being short is misfortune. If you laugh at a short joke you're just being mean.

Humor rewards you for learning about things you can avoid – like mistakes – but not for things you can't avoid – like misfortune.

2. You only feel humor when a mistake is rank-reducing.

You don't feel humor if you learn about a mistake that doesn't lower somebody's rank. It's funny to learn, for example, about a normally sober person getting drunk and making an ass of themselves. It's not funny to learn about a habitual drunkard getting drunk and making an ass of themselves. The normally sober person reduced their rank. The habitual drunk did not.

3. You only feel humor if you can make the same mistake.

Said alternatively, you do not feel humor if you cannot make the same mistake. Men find jokes about erectile dysfunction funny, but not jokes about menstrual cramping. Women find jokes about bras funny, but not jokes about jock itch.

Humor only rewards you for learning about mistakes you could make. If you can't make a particular mistake, you don't gain by learning about it.

Tabloid newspapers have learned this lesson. The gossip that sells the most newspapers focusses on famous women who are overweight or cheating. Those are the mistakes their target audience is most likely to make.

4. You only feel humor when a mistake is news to you.

A joke is not funny the second time you hear it. You don't feel humor the second time because you're not learning something new. Humor only rewards you for learning something new. If you're not learning something new, you're not rewarded.

Punchlines, twists and the element of surprise are the something new that makes jokes work. They teach you something you didn't know or know enough to connect.

The more likely you are to make the same mistake, the stronger humor feels.

If there is no possibility you could make the same mistake described in a joke, you won't feel humor – as just described above. If there is a low probability you could make the same mistake, you'll feel weak humor. If there is a high probability you could make the same mistake, you'll feel strong humor.

People who have recently stopped smoking or drinking are usually the first to criticize others for smoking or drinking – because they feel strong humor when they do. They are the people most likely to make the mistake of smoking or drinking. For similar reasons, people on diets are usually the first to criticize others for being fat.

Your fears are revealed by what you find funny, gossip about or criticize.
Your humor is strongest for mistakes you're most likely to make. So you're subconsciously attracted to jokes, gossip and criticism that involves mistakes you're most likely to make.

You can learn what mistakes you most fear making by remembering which moments of humor, gossip or criticism stick out as memorable. If you remember gossiping about a co-worker caught shopping online at work, you're probably worried about being caught doing the same.

A particularly good moment to see the subconscious effect of humor is when you change the subject of a casual conversation. You usually change to subjects that make you feel strong humor – a particularly good bit of gossip, for example. If the gossip makes you feel such strong humor that you wanted to change the subject to talk about it, you probably have a strong fear of making the same mistake that you're gossiping about.

Other's fears are revealed by what they find funny, gossip about or criticize.
Like you, the humor that others feel is strongest for mistakes they're most likely to make. So they're subconsciously attracted to jokes, gossip and criticism that involves mistakes they're most likely to make.

As with you, a particularly good moment to see the subconscious effect of humor on others is when they change the subject of casual conversations. Their subject choices reflect their fears. If a man often jokes about homosexuals, he's probably gay or considering it. If a woman frequently gossips about alcoholics, she's probably worried about being an alcoholic.

Tell jokes and gossip about mistakes your audience could make.
Don't use your gut to evaluate whether your audience will enjoy a joke or gossip. Your humor is strongest for mistakes you could make. Your audience's humor is strongest for mistakes they could make – which are often different than yours.

Don't tell elderly people, for example, jokes about sending a mistyped text message. Instead, tell them jokes about not hearing what somebody said or being incontinent. Don't tell teenagers, for example, gossip about adults who cheated on their taxes. Instead, tell them gossip about other teenagers cheating on their boyfriends or girlfriends.

Writers and editors have a bias towards mistakes they could make.
Writers and editors use their gut to decide how good a joke or story is. They assume their reaction will be the same as their audience's reaction. This is a mistake. Jokes and stories that are most appealing to writers and editors are about mistakes they're most likely to make – which are often different than the mistakes their audience are most likely to make.

News editors, for example, give too much prominence to scandals involving other new organizations. The telephone hacking scandal involving Rupert Murdoch's UK newspapers, for example, was a top news story in 2011. It was particularly enjoyable for news editors, but it wasn't gossip their readers would enjoy – their readers aren't likely to be caught hacking telephones.

Seek comedy that focuses on mistakes that you could make.
Comedic entertainment, such as movies or stand-up acts, that focus on mistakes you could make will make you feel the strongest humor. The Hangover movie series focussed on mistakes men could make. Bridesmaids was focused on mistakes women could make.

Comedy businesses should explicitly market the mistakes they focus on.
The more explicitly a comedy business describes the mistakes it will focus on, the easier it is for customers to evaluate how funny it will be for them. If the focus is on mistakes they could make, they'll be happy patrons. If the focus is not on mistakes they could make, they'll avoid being unhappy patrons.

The Blue Collar Tour and Larry The Cable Guy did particularly well because they explicitly targeted the largest segment of mistake makers – middle-class people worried about being low class.

Humor causes the mistake of criticizing others.
Criticizing others is a mistake. When you criticize somebody you lower their rank which makes them feel humiliation. Unless they asked for the criticism, they will then feel revenge. And that person will always feel revenge towards you unless they get you back. Unsolicited criticism creates enemies – and for what benefit?

People criticize others because it makes them feel humor – but they don't realize it. Instead, they think they're helping the other person. Parents, for example, criticize their children using the rationale they're "sharing their experience". The real reason is because it makes them feel humor.

Expect others to criticize you.
If you realize that we're all programmed to enjoy criticizing each other, you won't take it personally when you become the target of somebody's criticism.

Resist the urge to defend yourself. You'll get into an argument and rob yourself of an opportunity to learn about yourself.

And resist the urge to criticize the other person because their criticism has made you feel revenge. Criticizing them will then cause them to feel humiliation and revenge and escalate the discussion to a confrontation.

The best reaction to being criticized is to <u>just listen</u> and let the conversation move on to a new subject. And replace friends who can't resist the urge to criticize you.

The safest humor describes your mistakes.
To be funny, humor must reduce somebody's rank. If humor reduces your rank, you avoid creating enemies and still make others feel humor.

The Three Stooges and Rodney Dangerfield make people laugh by acting out or describing their mistakes.

" As a child, I got no respect.
When I played in the sandbox, the cat kept covering me up."

Witty jokes and putdowns make you feel humor and pride.
Witty jokes and putdowns differ from regular jokes and putdowns because they include insights.

We prefer witty jokes and putdowns because they make us feel two emotions – humor and pride. The joke or putdown makes us feel humor. Recognizing the insight elevates our rank to the comedian's rank – which makes us feel pride.

" President Bush is waging war for the sake of the environment.
He hopes to drive the price of oil so high that we stop driving cars."

" You're a waste of carbon. "

Puns make you feel pride, but not humor.
Like witty jokes, puns make you feel pride because recognizing their play on words elevates your rank. However, they don't make you feel humor because they don't describe a mistake that lowers someone's rank.

" I used to be a gold prospector,
but it didn't pan out."

Humor seems stronger when it also stops envy.
If you envy somebody, it's more enjoyable to learn about them make a rank-reducing mistake. Their mistake simultaneously makes you feel humor and stops you feeling envy.

The tall-poppy syndrome is an example. People prefer to criticize tall-poppies because it makes them feel humor and stops their envy. The most vocal critics of tall-poppies are their former peers – the people who envy them most.

Chapter 12
Revenge & Anger

You start feeling revenge when somebody harms you by breaking the rules.
You start feeling the negative effect of revenge, for example, when:
- somebody cuts you off while you're driving
- somebody cuts in front of you in a line-up
- somebody spreads rumors about you
- somebody intentionally injures you
- somebody steals from you

Revenge requires rule breaking.
You don't feel revenge if somebody harms you without breaking the rules.

You feel revenge if you're bumped by a stranger as you walk down the street, but not if you're bumped by another player in a contact sport. The stranger broke the rules of etiquette, the other player did not.

You feel revenge if another driver cuts you off, but not if you're cut off by an ambulance with its lights flashing. The other driver broke the rules of safe driving, the ambulance did not .

The more a rule breaker harms you, the stronger revenge feels.
If a robber forces you to give him your wallet, you'll feel moderate revenge. If the robber also gives you a black eye, you'll feel much stronger revenge.

The stronger revenge is, the more likely you are to retaliate. You're more likely to report a robber that also gives you a black eye.

You stop feeling revenge when you retaliate against the rule breaker.
You stop feeling revenge, for example, when:
- you yell a profanity at somebody who cut you off
- you publicly shame somebody for cutting in a line-up
- you spread rumors about somebody who spread rumors about you
- you injure somebody who intentionally injured you
- you have somebody who stole from you charged with theft

After the negative effect of revenge stops, you don't feel good – you just stop feeling bad. If somebody harms you, you enjoy getting them back because it stops you feeling a negative – not because it makes you feel a positive.

Revenge doesn't stop until you achieve eye-for-an-eye retaliation.
If another driver cuts you off in traffic, they've caused you minor harm. Yelling a profanity at the other driver will be sufficient to stop your revenge – it causes the other driver a similar degree of harm. If a drunk driver leaves you handicapped, yelling a profanity won't be enough to stop your revenge. The drunk driver will need to serve many years in jail to stop your revenge.

The need for eye-for-an-eye retaliation determines how much you retaliate. You keep feeling revenge until you've harmed the rule breaker as much as the rule breaker harmed you.

Eye-for-an-eye retaliation delivers the optimal punishment. It punishes rule breakers enough to deter future rule breaking, but it doesn't punish rule breakers more than necessary. Two-eyes-for-an-eye punishment would not deter rule breakers significantly more, but would cause significantly more harm to the rule breaker and the person retaliating.

If you don't retaliate, revenge doesn't stop.
If you don't get someone back, you'll keep feeling revenge towards them – you will feel <u>unstopped revenge</u>. Everybody holds grudges. Everybody can still remember people who have harmed them years ago. They remember these grudges and people because they still feel unstopped revenge.

Don Rickles was asked how his friend Frank Sinatra was doing given that Frank was getting older and was rumored to be losing his memory. Rickles responded by saying "Oh, he's got Sicilian Alzheimer's. He only remembers the grudges."

Forgiving doesn't stop revenge. You can decide to forgive somebody, but it won't stop you feeling revenge. That can only be stopped by retaliating.

People often deal with unstopped revenge by harming innocent people.
At a given moment, many people feel unstopped revenge. Many people are frequently in situations where they are harmed by a rule breaker and cannot retaliate. Two big sources are bosses and parents.

Bosses often mistreat their employees. They humiliate them with criticism or jokes, for instance. And employees cannot retaliate without losing their jobs. So employees accumulate more unstopped revenge with each day of humiliation. And then they go home.

Employees often deal with their unstopped revenge by harming family. Parents feeling unstopped revenge have disproportionate responses, for example, to the tiniest rule breaking. A child accidentally breaks a glass and the father flies into a rage striking his child. The unstopped revenge then gets transferred to the child.

Pet abusers, bullies and haters are motivated by unstopped revenge. When they harm others, they stop their unstopped revenge and their unhappiness. They pick victims that can't fight back – pets, smaller people or posting anonymously. This can only partially stop their unstopped revenge – they're not retaliating against the people who made them feel revenge.

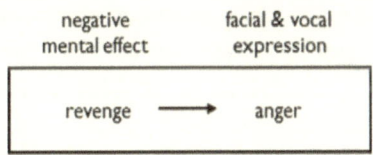

People often express anger when they feel revenge.
Revenge is a negative mental effect. Anger is a facial and vocal expression. Anger typically includes yelling, screaming, profanity, threatening, hand waving, furled brows and glaring.

Anger is a <u>voluntary</u> expression. People can choose to not express anger when they feel revenge – when their boss insults them, for example. And people can choose to express anger when they don't feel revenge – mothers trying to control their children, for example.

Anger seems to be an involuntary reaction to revenge because it's a deeply ingrained habit, like walking or talking. You don't think about walking or talking – you just do it out of habit. Similarly, you don't think about getting angry – you just get angry out of habit when you feel revenge.

Anger is just one form of retaliation.
There is a spectrum of behaviors that people use to retaliate. Anger is at the nice end of the spectrum. The more somebody harms you, the more harmful your retaliation will be. If you insulted me, I'll probably just give you the cold shoulder. If you cut me off in traffic, I'll probably express anger by yelling a profanity at you. If you're a business partner who stole from me, I'll probably sue you. If you harm me physically, I'll probably use violence to get you back.

It helps to realize that revenge makes you self-destructive.
Revenge makes you want to harm people. It also makes you willing to harm yourself to do it. It would be logical to wonder if you're broken if you want to cause such harm – particularly when you're imagining assaulting others. Why would you want to do something that is so obviously self-destructive?

Don't worry. You're normal if you want to hurt people who made you mad. Everybody is programmed by revenge to retaliate against rule breakers. And it makes you want to retaliate even when it harms you. Revenge specifically evolved to overcome your rationale conclusion that most retaliation is bad for you. By encouraging you to always retaliate, revenge deters rule breaking. That helps your group be more efficient, but makes you self-destructive.

Realizing that revenge is normal makes it easier to manage. You don't, for example, pursue solutions that assume you're broken – like pharmaceuticals or therapy. Instead, the best approach is to think of revenge as a bit of malware we all have inside our heads. If you're aware of it, you can minimize the harm it causes you – as described on the following pages.

Minimizing revenge will make you happier and more successful.
Your ability to minimize the harm that revenge causes you will make a big difference to everything. You'll avoid getting into conflicts that often end up in courts or hospitals. You'll be more successful with family and work. Everybody prefers people who can keep their cool and are not habitually angry. Most importantly, you won't be plagued by revenge – a prime source of unhappiness for many.

Revenge is best minimized by:
1. avoiding revenge situations
2. avoiding the revenge conclusion
3. doing and saying nothing
4. retaliating after thoughtful planning

1. First, avoid revenge situations.
By far, the easiest way to minimize revenge is to avoid revenge situations – situations that you know are likely to make you feel revenge. Parking near the entrance of supermarkets is an example of a revenge situation. The parking spots near entrances are usually filled and you're likely to encounter somebody who parks too close to your car or dents your car with their door. You can avoid these situations by parking away from the entrance where there are many empty spots.

2. If you can't avoid revenge situations, avoid the revenge conclusion.
You feel revenge when you conclude that someone harmed you and they did it by breaking the rules. If you can re-interpret somebody's behavior as <u>not harmful</u> or <u>not rule breaking</u>, then you won't feel revenge.

An example are drivers who change lanes without signalling. They harm you by increasing the risk of an accident. And they break the rules of safe driving. These two conclusions make you feel revenge.

There are two ways you could avoid reaching the revenge conclusion by re-interpreting their behavior. First, you could conclude that other driver did not harm you because you expect lane changes without signalling. This would be case if not signalling becomes so common that nobody is surprised when it happens. Second, you could conclude that unwritten rules of the road say it's okay to not signal. This would be the case if not signalling becomes so commonplace that it becomes tolerated behavior.

This approach applies to the limited number of situations where there is more than one way to interpret the situation. And it's of limited success in these situations – it's difficult to stop your mind reverting to the initial conclusions which made you feel revenge.

3. If you cannot avoid feeling revenge, do and say nothing.
The best way to do nothing is to develop the habit of doing nothing. The only way to resist revenge is to have a response that doesn't require any thinking. If you have to think about how to respond when you're feeling revenge, revenge will overcome your rationale thoughts and make you retaliate. A habit bypasses the need to think.

The habit of doing nothing should replace the habit of expressing anger. Most people let themselves develop the habit of expressing anger when they feel revenge. This habit can be undone and replaced by doing nothing, but it's hard work – like quitting smoking or changing your accent.

The habit of doing nothing applies to both actions and words – say nothing. When feeling revenge, it's impossible to have a constructive conversation. They always descend into an insulting exchange that makes things worse and sometimes escalates to violence. It's weird to say nothing while somebody yells at you, but it's always better in the long run – especially with strangers. If you must say something, then say you're very upset right now and want to cool down before responding – and then walk away.

Doing and saying nothing is much easier if you don't imagine doing or saying anything. People always imagine how they'll retaliate before they do – often repeatedly. So when they feel a surge of revenge, they impulsively follow the images of retaliation that have become ingrained in their minds. This is when people claim they acted without thinking and can't explain their behavior. They did think about what they did – not when they did it, but many times before they did it.

Instead of imagining retaliating, imagine doing and saying nothing. And then do nothing when revenge surges. If you do nothing when feeling revenge, you'll feel pride the first few times you do it.

If you do nothing, you'll be left feeling unstopped revenge. It may lead you to harm an innocent person or retaliate disproportionately to minor rule breaking. Being aware of your unstopped revenge will help you avoid taking it out on others.

4. If you must retaliate, do it after thoughtful planning.
In some circumstances, you won't be able to resist retaliating. If you've been seriously harmed by blatant rule breaking, you may so preoccupied by your feelings of revenge that you cannot enjoy life. In these situations, you should retaliate.

However, you should not retaliate impulsively. Your initial reaction to feeling revenge should always be do and say nothing. Then take your time to think about how to retaliate at minimal cost to you. This is what is meant by the saying "revenge is a dish best served cold". You should retaliate after you've thought about the method of retaliation that harms you least. Instead of tailgating a reckless driver, for example, give a video of his driving to the police.

You should worry about people who feel revenge towards you.
People who feel revenge towards you are programmed to harm you even if it harms them. They will, for instance, key your car if they think you took their parking spot. They'll risk a criminal charge just to stop feeling mild revenge.

And if somebody also felt unstopped revenge before you made them feel revenge, you could receive a disproportionate response. When somebody goes postal, it's because a small incident unleashes years of unstopped revenge that can only stopped by being very harmful to others – including murder.

Saying sorry is a smart way to stop another person's revenge.
Everyone knows that saying sorry makes the apologist feel humiliation. That's why it stops people feeling revenge – it's painful for the rule breaker to say. And that pain provides the eye-for-eye retaliation a victim needs to stop feeling revenge.

Saying sorry is a particularly good way of dealing with irate strangers. Saying sorry turns off their revenge like a switch. Try it sometime. You will be pleasantly surprised. So will the irate person.

If you do say sorry, never qualify it. Don't start your apology, for example, with "if I offended anyone". While it reduces the humiliation you feel, it undercuts the apology for victims who feel revenge. As a result, the apology doesn't stop their revenge.

When sorry is not enough, you should consider offering self-punishment.
In situations where you've caused substantial harm, saying sorry will not be enough. Even if you apologize, your victim will continue to feel revenge.

If the person is somebody you'll interact with again, you have to worry about this – particularly if you'll be interacting with them frequently, such as a family member or co-worker. If you don't stop their revenge, the other person will retaliate by being uncooperative or passive aggressive. The relationship will be acrimonious.

To avoid these outcomes, it may be wise to offer more than just saying sorry.

For example, if you failed to check on your brother's dog while he was away and it died, saying sorry will probably not stop his revenge. To stop it, you could give him a large payment that acts like the fine a criminal would pay.

For another example, if you disclosed to others that a co-worker has an STD, saying sorry will probably not stop your co-worker's revenge. To stop it, you could tell the co-worker to reveal to others that you have a DUI conviction.

Chapter 13
Criminal Guilt

You feel criminal guilt when you harm someone by breaking the rules.
You feel criminal guilt, for example, when you:
- steal money from somebody
- hit a bicyclist when running a red light
- knock somebody down while texting and walking
- cause permanent injury to somebody while driving drunk
- kill someone against their wishes

You have to break rules to feel criminal guilt.
If you harm someone without breaking the rules, you don't feel criminal guilt.

You'll feel criminal guilt if you run a red light and hit a bicyclist, but not if a bicyclist runs a red light and you hit him. You break the rules when you run a red light, but not when a bicyclist runs a red light.

You'll feel criminal guilt if you knock somebody down while texting and walking, but not if you knock somebody down while playing a contact sport. You break the rules of etiquette when you knock someone down while texting, but not when playing a contact sport.

You have to cause harm to feel criminal guilt.
If you break the rules without harming someone, you don't feel criminal guilt.

You don't feel criminal guilt, for example, if run a red light and don't hit anybody. And you don't feel criminal guilt if you text while walking and don't knock anybody down.

Criminals who commit victimless crimes, like drug users and prostitutes, don't feel criminal guilt. Nobody is harmed by their crimes.

Shoplifters avoid feeling criminal guilt by telling themselves their victim is a large corporation that will not be harmed by their petty theft.

People don't feel criminal guilt when they tell white lies. They're called white lies because they're believed to cause no harm. Telling a lie, for example, about why you were late for a meeting doesn't harm the person you met.

The more harm you caused, the stronger criminal guilt feels.
If you dent another car door when opening your door, you'll feel weak criminal guilt. If you permanently handicap someone while driving drunk, you'll feel much stronger criminal guilt.

If you steal $100 from a rich man, you'll feel weak criminal guilt. If you steal $100 from a homeless man, you'll feel much stronger criminal guilt.

The police often parade the crying relatives of murder victims in front of television cameras. They hope to increase the murderer's criminal guilt enough to turn himself in.

You never stop feeling criminal guilt.
Like grief, guilt is permanent. If you harm someone by breaking the rules, you'll always feel criminal guilt when you remember the incident or person.

You can't stop criminal guilt by confessing or being punished. Criminals often confess hoping that it will stop their criminal guilt – it doesn't. In addition to serving time, criminals still feel criminal guilt and have little to distract them from feeling it.

Being forgiven doesn't stop criminal guilt – unless it suggests no harm. If a victim states that you did not harm them, you'll stop feeling criminal guilt.

Criminal guilt can become a substantial source of unhappiness.
Each time you harm someone breaking the rules you're left feeling more criminal guilt forever. Those incidents accumulate in your head over the course of a lifetime. For older people who have wronged a lot of people, criminal guilt becomes a major source of unhappiness they cannot escape. Criminal guilt can become the equivalent of a chronic ailment that causes constant pain.

Chapter 14
Compassion

You start to feel compassion when you can help the unfortunate.

You start feeling the <u>negative</u> effect of compassion, for example, when you:

- see a double amputee on the sidewalk begging for money
- see somebody calling for help from a burning house
- see somebody knocked down by a falling tree
- see somebody abusing a weaker person
- see a dog running loose through traffic

Compassion requires the ability to help.

You don't feel compassion if you can't help an unfortunate person. Rich people feel compassion when they see the poor, for example, but poor people don't. Rich people can help the poor, but poor people can't.

You'll feel compassion if you see somebody fall to the ground in front of you, but not if you see somebody fall to the ground on *America's Funniest Home Videos*. You can't help the videotaped person.

Compassion requires the person be unfortunate.

If somebody needs help but isn't unfortunate, you don't feel compassion.

You feel compassion when you see a double-amputee begging for change, for example, but not when you see an able-bodied man begging for change.

You feel compassion when a single mother loses her house to a fire, but not when a billionaire loses one of his mansions to a fire.

The more harm you can prevent, the stronger compassion feels.

You'll feel strong compassion if you see an elderly man in a burning house. You'll feel even stronger compassion if you see a child in a burning house.

The stronger compassion is, the more likely you are to help somebody. You're more likely to save a child from a burning house than an elderly man. Saving a child would save more years of life.

You stop feeling compassion when you help the unfortunate.
You stop feeling the negative effect of compassion, for example, when you:
- give money to a double amputee on the sidewalk begging for money
- rescue somebody calling for help from a burning house
- call an ambulance for somebody knocked down by a falling tree
- stop somebody abusing a weaker person
- rescue a dog running loose through traffic

After the negative effect of compassion stops, you don't feel good – you just stop feeling bad. Heroes don't feel a positive effect after rescuing somebody. They just stop feeling the negative effect of compassion – until they start talking to the media. Then they start feeling pride.

The emotion of compassion motivates some compassionate behavior.
Compassion is an emotion and a behavior. While the emotion is a negative mental effect, the behavior is a positive contribution to a community.

Compassionate behavior can be separated into impulsive and planned. Impulsive compassionate behavior includes rescuing somebody from a fire or stopping a bully abusing somebody. Planned compassionate behavior includes donating money to charity or volunteering at a soup kitchen.

Impulsive compassionate behavior is primarily motivated by the emotion of compassion. A hero saves a child, for example, because he wants to stop feeling the negative mental effect of compassion.

Planned compassionate behavior is primarily motivated by the emotion of pride. People primarily donate money, for example, to feel the pride of being honored – not to stop feeling compassion.

The emotion of compassion is good for everybody, but bad for you.
Compassion is good for everybody. Because of compassion, we can rely on the kindness of strangers if we're unfortunate. This means we all need less insurance. You don't need, for example, to have an extra person with you when you travel. If you lose consciousness and fall to the ground, you can rely on strangers to call an ambulance.

Compassion is bad for you. When you help an unfortunate stranger, you could be harmed. If you rescue somebody from a fire, for example, you could be burned. If you help a man who appears to unconscious on the ground, you could be robbed.

Minimizing compassion will make you happiest.
Compassion is a negative emotion. The more you feel it, the less happy you will be. And it causes behavior that will distract you from feeling positive emotions. Compassion will drive you to spend time and money to help the unfortunate, which is good for society and bad for you. Instead, you could use the time and money to be with friends or go on vacations.

Compassion is best minimized by:
1. avoiding compassion situations
2. avoiding the compassion conclusion
3. doing nothing
4. helping on the condition that it's one-time

1. First, avoid compassion situations.
By far, the easiest way to avoid compassion is to avoid compassion situations – situations where you're likely to see unfortunate people that you could help. Don't, for example, go for walks on streets that have panhandlers. And turn the television channel when they air advertisements that show abused animals.

2. If you can't avoid compassion situations, avoid the compassion conclusion.
You feel compassion when you conclude you can prevent harm to an unfortunate person. If you can re-interpret the circumstances as one where you cannot help or the person is not unfortunate, you won't feel compassion.

This approach applies to the limited number of situations where there is more than one way to interpret the circumstances as cannot help or not unfortunate. And it's of limited success in these situations – it's difficult to stop your mind reverting to the initial conclusions which made you feel compassion. It would be difficult, for example, to stop feeling compassion for someone trapped in a fire because you learned the person is an arsonist.

3. If you can't avoid feeling compassion, do nothing.

The best way to do nothing is to develop the <u>habit</u> of doing nothing. The only way to resist compassion is to have a response that doesn't require any thinking. If you have to think about how to respond when you're feeling compassion, compassion will overcome your rationale thoughts and make you help. A habit bypasses the need to think.

If you do nothing, you'll feel selfish guilt – see next chapter.

4. If you must help the unfortunate, do it on the condition that it's one-time.

In some circumstances, you won't be able to do nothing. If you're confronted with a situation where you can prevent serious harm, you may be so preoccupied by your feelings of compassion that you can't enjoy life. In these situations, you should help.

However, you should only help after the unfortunate person agrees not to ask for more. If you fail to do this, you run the risk of creating a lifelong problem. Even if you secure their agreement, the unfortunate person will probably come back for more help. The agreement makes it easier to say no when they do.

Obviously, adding conditions to your help does not apply to emergencies – like rescuing somebody from a fire. It only applies to non-emergencies, like loaning somebody money.

Chapter 15
Selfish Guilt

You feel selfish guilt when you fail to help the unfortunate.
You feel selfish guilt, for example, if you <u>do nothing</u> when you:
- see a double amputee on the sidewalk begging for money
- see somebody calling for help from a burning house
- see somebody knocked down by a falling tree
- see somebody abusing a weaker person
- see a dog running loose through traffic

Like compassion, selfish guilt requires ability to help.
If you couldn't have prevented harm to an unfortunate person, you don't feel selfish guilt.

You feel selfish guilt if you do nothing when you see somebody knocked down in front of you, but not when you see somebody knocked down on America's Funniest Videos. You could've helped the person in front of you, but not the person on America's Funniest Videos.

People try to avoid feeling selfish guilt by telling themselves they couldn't help. The friends of suicide victims, for example, tell each other there were no signs of depression. If there were no signs, friends couldn't have known their help was needed – so they don't feel selfish guilt.

Like compassion, selfish guilt requires misfortune.
If somebody needed help but was not unfortunate, you don't feel selfish guilt.

You feel selfish guilt if you do nothing when you see a double amputee begging for money, but not if you do nothing when you see an able-bodied man begging for money.

The more harm you could have prevented, the stronger selfish guilt feels.
You'll feel moderate selfish guilt, for example, if you drive by a stranded motorist gesturing for help. You'll feel much stronger selfish guilt if the motorist dies of exposure that night.

Selfish guilt is permanent.

Like grief, you never stop feeling selfish guilt. Every time you think of a person you didn't help, you'll feel selfish guilt. And those memories can accumulate over a lifetime to become a substantial source of unhappiness later in life.

Survivor's guilt is proof that selfish guilt is permanent. Many decades after a war or genocide, survivors still express guilt for "not doing more" to help those that did not survive. Feeling that selfish guilt often makes survivors release suppressed crying.

criminal guilt	selfish guilt
you harm someone by breaking the rules	you don't help an unfortunate person

Criminal guilt and selfish guilt are different emotions.

While both are negative emotions you feel when somebody else is harmed, they are caused by different situations. You feel criminal guilt when you harm someone by breaking the rules. You feel selfish guilt when you fail to help an unfortunate person.

You feel criminal guilt, for example, when you set someone's house on fire. You feel selfish guilt when you fail to tell someone their house is on fire.

Simply put, criminal guilt is about breaking the rules, and selfish guilt is about not helping the unfortunate.

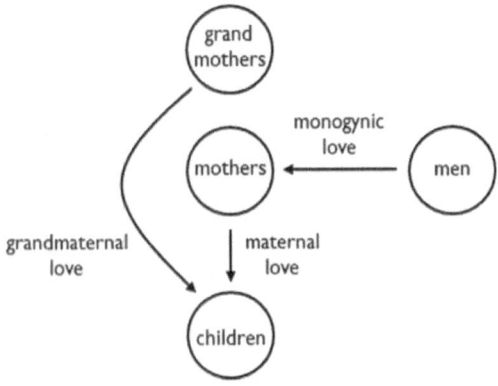

Only three people feel love.
- mothers love their children
- grandmothers love their grandchildren
- men love their women

Nobody else feels love.
- fathers don't love their children
- grandfathers don't love their grandchildren
- children don't love their parents
- siblings don't love their siblings
- friends don't love their friends
- pet owners don't love their pets

Love creates three parent post-natal care, but not more.
Love is a strong emotion felt when a loved person is happy. It causes the loving person to harm their survival by diverting resources and taking risks to make the loved person happy. Because love is so biologically expensive, it only applies to the three people most important to raising a child – the mother, grandmother and father.

Other people are genetically related to a child, but can't provide help that isn't already provided by the mother, grandmother and father. Mothers feed children. Fathers feed mothers. Grandmothers provide experience.

Everybody else feels affection, not love.
Affection feels like a weaker form of love. You feel it when you see or hear people that are close to you.

In addition to being weaker than love, affection motivates people differently. You only feel love when you conclude that your loved one is happy. You feel affection when you see or hear familiar people – whether they're happy or not. While love makes you want somebody's happiness, affection just makes you just want their presence.

Everybody feels cute when they see infants.
The sight of infants makes everyone feel the positive sensation of cute. Fathers feel it when they see their newborn children and mistakenly think it's paternal love. Grandfathers mistakenly think it's grandpaternal love.

Recognizing that many relationships are not based on love would be helpful.
Recognizing that fathers don't love their children would be helpful. Fathers, for example, can stop feeling guilty about not sharing their wives' enthusiasm for their children. Instead, fathers can focus on what makes them happiest, which is usually feeling pride from career success.

Recognizing that grandfathers don't love their grandchildren would be helpful. Grandmothers, for example, will be more understanding if they know their husbands don't share their enthusiasm about a new grandchild. It's not a sign that he's cold or uncaring – he just doesn't feel love like grandmothers do.

Recognizing that children don't love their parents would be helpful. Parents, for example, won't be disappointed when their adult children spend little with them. And knowing that children are unlikely to be a reliable source of companionship means parents will count on friends for companionship instead.

Recognizing that siblings don't love each other would be helpful. Parents, for example, won't feel like failures because their children don't get along – children aren't supposed to get along. Siblings, for example, will not waste their time trying to make a troublesome sibling relationship work because they think it's underpinned by love. Sibling relationships are no stronger than friendships. If they don't work, you should move on.

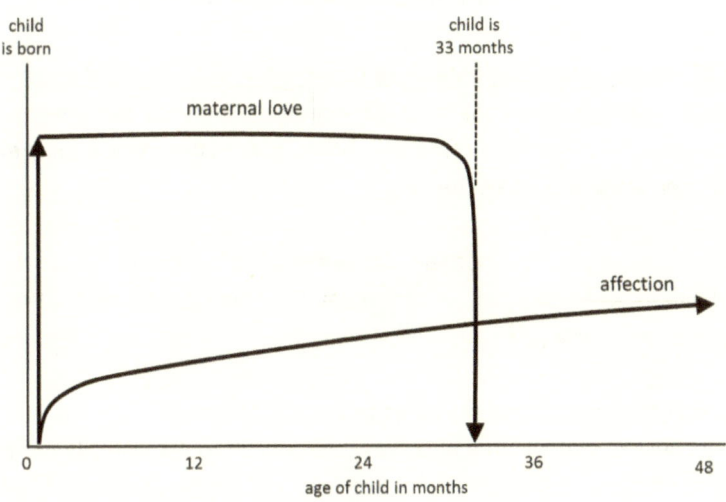

Mothers feel maternal love when their child is happy.
And the happier a child is, the stronger maternal love feels.

Mothers stop feeling maternal love when a child is 33 months old.
Mothers start feeling maternal love when their child is born and stop feeling it when their child is 33 months old – which is when a child's first set of teeth have fully erupted.

In the past, before baby formula and Gerber food, children needed assistance to eat before their teeth fully erupted. Mothers breastfed them or transferred masticated food to their children through mouth-to-mouth contact.

Once a child's first set of teeth have fully erupted at 33 months, a child can eat without assistance if given food. At that point, a child no longer needs the full-time attention of his mother. Maternal love for the current child stops at 33 months of age to prepare mothers for the next child.

After 33 months, mothers continue to feel affection.
Mothers do continue to feel the weaker positive effect of affection when they see or hear their children, which they mistakenly believe is maternal love.

In addition to being weaker than maternal love, affection motivates mothers differently. Love rewards mothers when their child is happy. Affection rewards mothers when they see or hear their child – whether their child is happy or not.

After 33 months, mothers continue to face the threat of maternal grief.
Although maternal love ends after 33 months, the threat of maternal grief never ends. If a child dies before its mother, the mother feels grief – even if the children are adults when they die.

Maternal grief motivates mothers, for example, to make sure their children wear helmets when bicycling. Mothers say they take these steps out of love, but it's really to avoid grief.

The end of maternal love contributes to the terrible-two's.
Mothers believe that children become more difficult to manage when they are 24-36 months old. While this is true, mothers' perception of their children also changes during this period. At 33 months, mothers stop feeling the very pleasurable reward of maternal love. It suddenly becomes much less enjoyable to manage a child.

Children do become more difficult at 24 months. At that age, they begin to feel the emotions of revenge, compassion, guilt, pride, humiliation, envy and humor. This is when they start having tantrums, for example, because they now feel revenge.

Mothers should expect the end of maternal love.
Mothers should expect their happiness to decline when their children are 33 months old. If they do, they won't mistakenly attribute their unhappiness to the wrong cause and take incorrect actions. They will not, for example, conclude they are depressed or need pharmaceutical help. They will not conclude that they need a new career, house or husband.

Having another child is a common reaction to the end of maternal love. Mothers can feel continuous maternal love if they have another child when the current child is 33 months old. This comes to an end when the last child is 33 months old. At that point, the mother is as unhappy as she would be if she had stopped at one child – but now she has the burden of multiple children.

Prospective mothers should consider the limited duration of maternal love.
Prospective mothers choose to have a child because they believe that the "joy of motherhood" outweighs the many costs of having a child. They see the "joy of motherhood" on the beaming faces of new mothers and want to feel it themselves. The "joy of motherhood" is the joy of maternal love.

Prospective mothers mistakenly assume they'll feel the "joy of motherhood" or maternal love forever. They assume it will always be there to offset the ongoing costs of children. And children are appealing when you make this mistaken assumption.

Prospective mothers should assume maternal love stops at 33 months, leaving only affection and maternal grief. And their children will only feel affection for them, not love. And siblings don't love each other – which adds to work of managing multiple children. These assumptions provide a realistic view of what having a child means to happiness. Biology fools mothers into a lifelong commitment using the short term reward of maternal love.

Infatuation is temporarily suppressed during pregnancy and maternal love.
Mothers do not feel infatuation while they are pregnant and for the 33 months of maternal love that follow. Infatuation's suppression keeps mothers focussed on their children. Mothers start feeling infatuation again when their child is 33 months old to encourage mothers to have another child with another man.

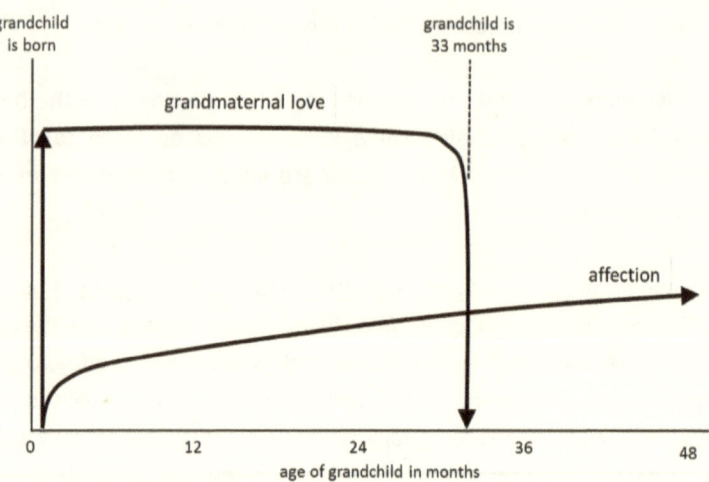

Grandmothers feel grandmaternal love when their grandchild is happy.
And the happier a grandchild is, the stronger grandmaternal love feels. Grandmaternal love is very similar to maternal love.

Grandmothers stop feeling love when a grandchild is 33 months old.
Grandmothers start feeling grandmaternal love when their grandchild is born and stop feeling it when their grandchild is 33 months old. Grandmaternal love stops at 33 months, when a grandchild can eat without assistance, to prepare grandmothers for the next grandchild.

After 33 months, grandmothers continue to feel affection.
Grandmothers do continue to feel the weaker positive effect of affection when they see or hear their grandchildren which they mistakenly believe is grandmaternal love.

In addition to being weaker than grandmaternal love, affection motivates grandmothers differently. Grandmaternal love rewards grandmothers when their grandchild is happy. Affection rewards grandmothers when they see or hear their grandchild – whether their grandchild is happy or not.

After 33 months, grandmothers continue to face the threat of grief.
Although grandmaternal love ends at 33 months, the threat of grandmaternal grief never ends. If a grandchild dies before its grandmother, the grandmother feels grief – regardless of the grandchild's age.

Love causes helpful conflict between mothers and grandmothers.
Love does not cause conflict between mothers and fathers. They don't love the same person. Mothers love their children and fathers love the mother of their children. Mothers want to make their child happy and fathers want to make their child's mother happy.

Love does cause conflict between mothers and grandmothers. They both love the child. So they compete to make the child happy. The resulting competition helps the child by delivering the best of both – the energy of the mother and the wisdom of the grandmother.

Chapter 19
Cute

You feel cute when you see scaled-down versions of things, like infants.
Infants make you feel cute because they are scaled-down versions of adults. Parents have newborn hands and feet bronzed to preserve that feeling of cute. Cute evolved to make you like infants – more attention helps their survival.

Anything that's scaled down can make you feel cute. Puppies and kittens make you feel cute because they're scaled down dogs and cats. Mini Coopers make you feel cute because they're scaled down cars.

Cute is stronger when a scaled-down version is beside a full-size version. A baby elephant is cuter when it's beside an adult elephant.

Fathers mistake cute as paternal love.
Fathers believe they feel paternal love when they see their infant children. They don't feel love – they feel cute. There are two key differences between cute and maternal love, for comparison.

First, fathers feel cute whether their infant child is happy or not. Mothers only feel maternal love if their child is happy. Fathers, for example, tolerate crying babies longer than mothers. When babies cry, fathers don't stop feeling love but mothers do.

Second, fathers only feel cute while looking at their infant children. Mothers feel maternal love whether they're looking at their child or not. While fathers like seeing their children, mothers like having children.

Cute stops when an infant is 33 months old.
Infants make you feel the strongest cute when they're newborns. As they get older and less scaled-down, they make you feel weaker cute. It stops entirely by the time they're 33 months old. By that age, they need less attention and are familiar enough to make others feel moderately strong affection.

The end of cute also contributes to the terrible-two's. After 33 months, children seem like more trouble because their caregivers no longer feel cute when they see the children.

Cute is a minor, but easy source of happiness.
Cute is at best a moderately strong and brief source of happiness. It cannot match the highs associated with major emotions like pride, infatuation or love. But it is significant. A cute video is as enjoyable as a good joke.

Cute does not require much work. It's easy to find cute entertainment on television or the internet. It's easy to visit a pet store with puppies or kittens when shopping.

Cute does not have any downside. Eating to enjoy pleasing taste, for example, can lead to obesity. Exchanging gossip to enjoy humor, for example, can lead to quarreling. You can't enjoy too much cute.

Cute leads some people to buy pets they shouldn't.
People decide to buy pets while looking at puppies or kittens. They compare the cute they feel while looking at the puppy or kitten against the ongoing costs of a pet. Then they buy the pet mistakenly assuming they'll always feel cute when they look at their pet. Unfortunately, many pets become more of a burden than a benefit when they stop being cute.

This problem is avoided if you buy an adult pet. If you like an adult pet when you see it in a shelter, you'll still like it in the future. There's no reason to think it will become less appealing – like a puppy or kitten will.

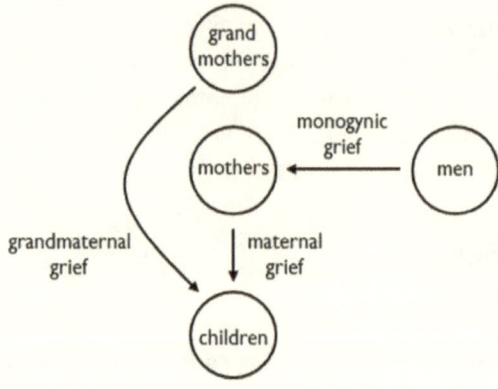

Only three people feel grief when someone dies.
- mothers feel grief when their children die
- grandmothers feel grief when their grandchildren die
- men feel grief when the women they love die

Other people don't feel grief when someone dies.
- fathers don't feel grief when their children die
- grandfathers don't feel when their grandchildren die
- children don't feel grief when their parents die
- siblings don't feel grief when their siblings die
- friends don't feel grief when their friends die
- pet owners don't feel grief when their pets die

Grief only punishes parents normally with their children.
Grief is a strong negative emotion felt when someone dies. The threat of feeling grief causes people to risk their survival to prevent someone's death. Because it's biologically expensive, it only affects parents who would normally be with their children. In the past, three parents were with a child until it was 33 months old – mothers, grandmothers and fathers. After 33 months, only two parents were normally with a child – mothers and grandmothers.

Men were not normally with their children after 33 months because they would have moved on to a new woman by then. And those men become grandfathers who were not with their grandchildren when they were born.

Everybody else feels imagined loneliness when someone dies, not grief.
When you picture an endless future without particular person, it makes you feel an emptiness. That emptiness is imagined loneliness.

Grief is much worse than imagined loneliness.
While grief and imagined loneliness are both negative emotions caused by death, they differ in two important ways.

First, grief is stronger than imagined loneliness – it's more emotionally painful. At a child's funeral, the mother and grandmother feel much worse than father, grandfather or siblings.

Second, grief is forever and imagined loneliness is not. Someone who feels grief will feel it whenever they think of the deceased. Someone who feels imagined loneliness only feels it while they imagine a future without the deceased. They can stop their imagined loneliness by simply imagining a future with other people. A grieving person can't do that.

Grief causes frowning.
When someone feels strong grief, they frown involuntarily – the corners of their mouth turn downwards in the opposite direction of a smile. It's the same expression you make when you feel disgust, but lasts longer.

Frowning is not a clear signal of grieving. People can voluntarily frown. And frowning from disgust can be confused with frowning from grieving.

Grief can cause crying, but only indirectly.
Crying is only caused by loneliness – real or imagined. Crying is often suppressed to be released later by any strong emotion, including grief. So grief can cause crying but only if the person was already lonely.

Crying and grief cannot be reliably connected. Crying doesn't mean somebody feels grief. And not crying doesn't mean somebody doesn't feel grief.

When someone dies, focus your concern on the grieving.
When dealing with the family and friends of somebody who died, focus your sympathy on those that feel grief – their mother, grandmothers and man if the deceased was a woman. These people are feeling more pain than anybody else. Everybody else is just feeling imagined loneliness.

Don't feel bad if you don't feel grief.
Unfortunately, it is incorrectly believed that everyone who is close to somebody will feel grief if they die. So you're expected to feel grief if somebody close to you dies. If you don't, others think you weren't close or aren't normal.

However, when someone close to you dies, you probably won't feel grief. The vast majority of the people who die before you will be your grandparents, parents, long-term partners and friends. None of these people will make you feel grief if they die before you.

Unless you're the mother, grandmother or boyfriend of the deceased, don't expect to feel grief. More importantly, don't question your humanity – you're normal.

Chapter 21
Maternal Grief

Mothers feel maternal grief when their children die.
Although maternal love stops when a child is 33 months old, the threat of maternal grief never stops. If their children die before them, mothers feel the stabbing pain of grief – even if the children are adults when they die.

Maternal grief is strongest when children die as teenagers.
The closer a child was to 16 years of age when they die, the stronger the maternal grief that a mother feels. Mothers of dead teenagers feel stronger grief than mothers of dead infants or mothers of dead adult children.

Grief encourages mothers to save their teenagers first. Teenagers have more reproductive potential than infants or adults.

Grieving mothers should avoid reminders of their dead children.
Mothers can't help their dead children by remembering them. Mothers can only inflict more pain on themselves by remembering. And the more grief that a mother feels, the less she can do for her remaining family. Although it seems callous, the best thing for a grieving mother and her family is to remove all reminders of a dead child. If necessary, the family might need to move.

Chapter 22
Grandmaternal Grief

Grandmothers feel grandmaternal grief when their grandchildren die.
Although grandmaternal love stops when a grandchild is 33 months old, the threat of grandmaternal grief never stops. If their grandchildren die before them, grandmothers feel the stabbing pain of grief – even if the grandchildren are adults when they die. Grandmaternal grief is similar to maternal grief.

Grandmaternal grief is strongest when grandchildren die as teenagers.
The closer a grandchild was to 16 years of age when they die, the stronger the grandmaternal grief that a grandmother feels. Grandmothers of dead teenagers feel stronger grief than grandmothers of dead infants or grandmothers of dead adult children.

Grieving grandmothers should avoid reminders of their dead grandchildren.
Grandmothers can't help their dead grandchildren by remembering them. Grandmothers can only inflict more emotional pain on themselves by remembering.

Chapter 23
Monogynic Grief

Men feel monogynic grief when the woman they love dies.
If a man loves a woman and she dies, he'll feel monogynic grief. And he'll always feel that grief when he thinks of her.

The longer a man has been in love, the stronger his grief.
Men who've been in love for three years feel stronger grief than men who've only been in love for a year.

Grief encourages men to risk more to save more advanced relationships. The longer a man has been in love, the greater the investment that is lost if his woman dies.

Men only feel grief if they're in love.
Men only feel grief if a woman dies during the 42 months of monogynic love. If a woman dies after a man has fallen out of love, he doesn't feel grief. Men in relationships that are at least 4 years old don't feel grief if their woman dies.

In the past, men would not normally be with a woman after 4 years. They would have fallen in love with another woman.

Grieving men should avoid reminders of their dead women.
Men cannot help their dead women by remembering them. Men can only inflict more pain on themselves by remembering.

Chapter 24
Male Sexual Pleasure

men	women
penile pleasure & orgasm	clitoral pleasure & orgasm
	vaginal pleasure
visual pleasure	
nipple pleasure	nipple pleasure

Men feel three types of sexual pleasure – penile, visual and nipple.
Men feel penile pleasure, which includes orgasm, from penile contact.

Men feel visual pleasure when they look at women. Visual pleasure is not as strong or discernible as penile pleasure. However, it's strong enough to cause men to spend billions on pornography and strip clubs. In addition, men must feel visual pleasure to fall in love with a woman, but not penile pleasure.

Men also feel nipple pleasure from nipple contact, but it's much weaker than penile pleasure and visual pleasure.

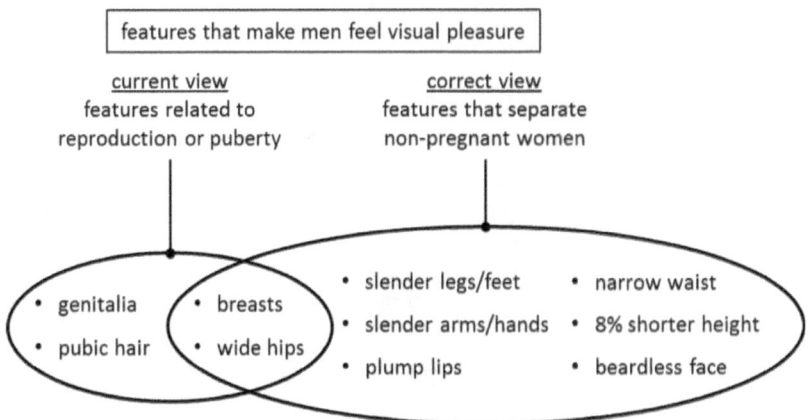

features that make men feel visual pleasure

current view
features related to
reproduction or puberty

correct view
features that separate
non-pregnant women

- genitalia
- pubic hair
- breasts
- wide hips
- slender legs/feet
- slender arms/hands
- plump lips
- narrow waist
- 8% shorter height
- beardless face

Visual pleasure is caused by features that separate non-pregnant women.
The current view is that men are turned on by features related to reproduction or puberty – such as genitalia, pubic hair, breasts and wide hips. This is only partially correct. The correct view is that men are turned on any feature that visually separates non-pregnant women from other humans.

Men are not turned on by the sight of genitalia or pubic hair. These features do not visually separate women from other humans. Female genitalia is normally hidden from view by pubic hair. And pubic hair does not separate women from men in particular – at least it didn't before Brazilian waxing.

Men are turned on by breasts and wide hips. Although these features are related to reproduction or puberty, they turn men on because they visually separate women from other humans.

Men are also turned on by slender legs/feet, slender arms/hands, plump lips, narrow waist, 8% shorter height and a beardless face. These features are not related to puberty or reproduction, but they do visually separate non-pregnant women. Slender legs/feet, slender arms/hands and plump lips separate women. A narrow waist separates non-pregnant women. To a man, 8% shorter height separates women from men and children. A beardless face separated women from men before men started shaving.

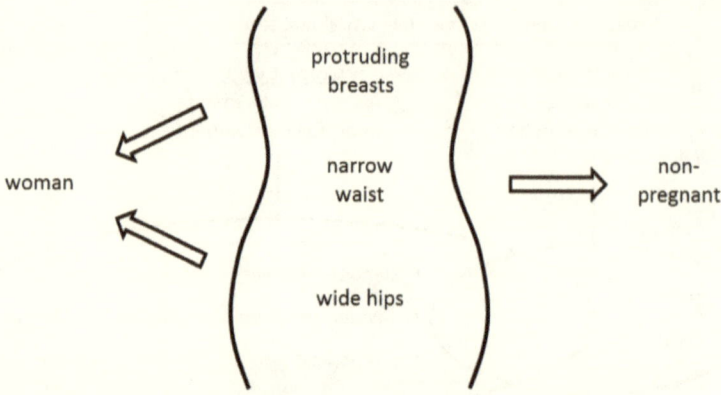

An hourglass figure makes men feel the strongest visual pleasure.

An hourglass figure is the combination of protruding breasts, a narrow waist and wide hips. This combination of features is the single visual that best confirms that somebody is a woman and non-pregnant.

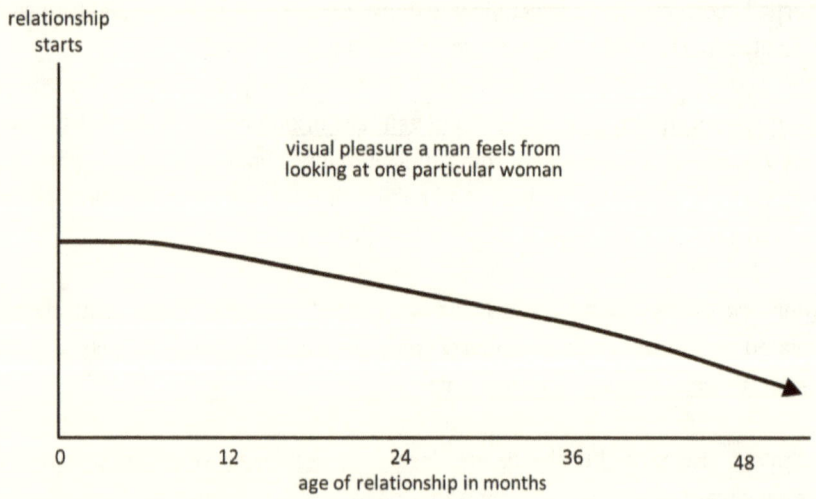

Visual pleasure declines with a woman's novelty.

The longer a man has known a woman, the weaker the visual pleasure he feels when he sees her. Women intuitively understand the importance of novelty. They wear a wide variety of new clothes to maximize their novelty. And they are keen to avoid wearing the same clothes as another woman.

94

Women should not expect to make a man feel strong visual pleasure for more than a year or two. Even if a woman is a supermodel, eventually her boyfriend will lose interest in looking her – but not novel women.

Men reach orgasm easier with visual pleasure.
Men can reach penile orgasm through penile contact alone. However, they find it much easier if they also feel visual pleasure – which feels best when looking at real women, but can also occur by remembering women. The linkage of visual pleasure to penile orgasm encourages men to prefer copulation over masturbation.

Men also feel visual pleasure when they see an erect penis.
Although it seems counter-intuitive, men do feel visual pleasure when they see an erect penis – theirs or another man's. It seems counter-intuitive because it seems to encourage homosexuality. However, it evolved long ago when our species engaged in multi-male mating – multiple males would mate with a single female one after another. Seeing the erect penises of other males would have stimulated males to prepare for this group mating.

The classic porn scene watched by heterosexual males, the money shot, is proof of this counter-intuitive aspect of visual pleasure. It commonly features an erect penis. If the sight of the erect penis did not make men feel visual pleasure, it wouldn't be the focus of the shot.

Feeling visual pleasure when looking at another man's erect penis has probably led men to believe they are homosexual.

The modern habit of shaving has also contributed to male homosexuality. Men evolved beards to stop men courting men – similar to the reason that male birds are marked by color and females are not. This made beardless faces a feature that separated women from men – and therefore makes men feel visual pleasure.

Men now feel visual pleasure when they look at the faces of women and the faces of men who shave.

Chapter 25
Lust

Lust is a behavior and a negative sensation.
Lust usually refers to the behavior of seeking sexual pleasure. Men lust after women for example.

Men lust after women because of a negative sensation that coerces them until they have sex. That negative sensation is also called lust in this book. The negative sensation of lust motivates lustful behavior.

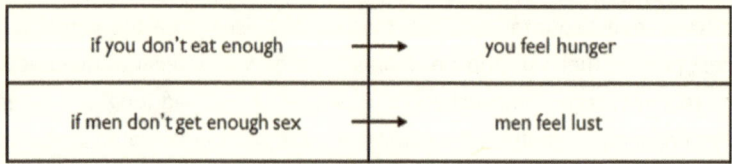

| if you don't eat enough | → | you feel hunger |
| if men don't get enough sex | → | men feel lust |

The sensation of lust works like hunger.
If you don't eat enough, you start feeling hunger. And the longer it's been since you've eaten, the stronger hunger becomes. Similarly, if men don't get enough sex, they start feeling lust. And the longer it's been since they've had sex, the stronger lust becomes.

Women do not feel lust.
It's one of the reasons women masturbate less than men. Women just masturbate to enjoy sexual pleasure. Men also masturbate to stop feeling lust. They accumulate stacks or files of pornography because they know that lust coerces them to seek ongoing sexual pleasure.

Only men feel lust because only men's genes gain from constantly having sex. Women's genes only gain from having sex when a man has just fallen in love with them – specifically during the four months of stage 2 infatuation.

Chapter 26
Repugnance

Men feel repugnance when they see or imagine their mother or sister naked.
Men feel the negative effect of repugnance when they feel visual pleasure while looking at a woman they lived with when they were 0-6 years old.

You can see evidence of repugnance when girls with brothers date other boys. Their brothers are uncomfortable because they know that other boys want to have sex with their sister. Imagining other boys having sex with their sister makes the brothers feel repugnance.

Women don't feel repugnance.
Evidence of this gender difference can be seen in the differing attitudes of siblings towards dating. While boys are uncomfortable with other boys dating their sisters, girls are completely comfortable with others girls dating their brothers. Girls often act as matchmaker setting up their friends with their brothers.

Women don't need to feel repugnance because men do. Only one gender needs to be discouraged to stop incest. However, women do have a natural brake against romantic family relations. They can only become infatuated with a stranger – so they can never become infatuated with fathers or brothers.

Fathers don't feel repugnance towards their daughters.
We assume that fathers feel repugnance towards daughters – it would prevent incest. However, they don't. In the distant past, fathers moved on to a new woman long before their daughters reached puberty. So there was no need for men to evolve repugnance towards their daughters.

This is real problem today – fathers are now typically with their daughters when they reach puberty. Fathers, mothers and daughters need to be aware of the risk of father-daughter attraction. Fathers should not be overly touchy with daughters. Daughters should dress conservatively around their fathers – for their father's benefit.

Brothers don't feel repugnance towards much younger sisters.
Specifically, they don't feel repugnance towards sisters that are 7 or more years younger than they are. Sisters this young were not alive when their older brother was 0-6 years old.

We assume that boys feel repugnance towards sisters of any age – it would prevent incest. However, they don't. In the distant past, brothers left their families looking for a mate before their much younger sisters reached puberty. So there was no need for brothers to evolve repugnance towards much younger sisters.

This could be a problem today – but only if an adult son is still living at home when his much younger sister reaches puberty. This would be a problem, for example, if a 21 year old son is living at home with his 14 year old sister. Repugnance will not discourage him from being sexually attracted to her.

Chapter 27
Female Sexual Pleasure

men	women
penile pleasure & orgasm	clitoral pleasure & orgasm
	vaginal pleasure
visual pleasure	
nipple pleasure	nipple pleasure

Women feel clitoral pleasure and orgasm.
Human embryos have the external parts for both sexes – all embryos have nipples, penises and scrotums. On men, the nipples do nothing and the penis and scrotum grow larger. On women, the nipples are pushed out by breasts and the penis and scrotum do nothing. The non-functioning penis is called a clitoris. The non-functioning scrotum is called labia.

Women have clitoral orgasms because they are really penile orgasms. The same wiring that gives men a penile orgasm gives women a clitoral orgasm.

Women feel vaginal pleasure, but not vaginal orgasm.
The only orgasm women feel is clitoral which can be mistaken as vaginal. During face-to-face intercourse, for example, men can stimulate a woman's clitoris. And the G-spot is just the lower structure of the clitoris when touched from inside the vagina.

Women don't feel vaginal orgasm because it's not needed for reproduction. Only men need to be rewarded for completing intercourse. Women just need to tolerate penetration, which is the purpose of vaginal pleasure.

Vaginal pleasure is elevated during the second stage of infatuation.

During the second 4 months of infatuation, women feel stronger vaginal pleasure and elevated vaginal lubrication. During this short window, women almost enjoy sex as much as men do.

Nipple pleasure is relatively weak.

While nipple pleasure can help women reach clitoral orgasm, it's weak compared to clitoral pleasure and orgasm. It's weak because it didn't evolve to encourage sex. It just encourages mothers to tolerate breastfeeding.

Women do not feel visual pleasure.

This gender difference can be seen in clothing choices. Men don't dress to be sexually attractive because they know it doesn't work. Women do dress to be sexually attractive because they know it does work. Men pay more attention when they wear low cut blouses, high heels, skirts or thongs.

This gender difference can also be seen in sex industries, such as pornography or strip clubs. The vast majority of their customers are men.

Women don't need to feel sexual pleasure because men do. Only one sex needs to be visually rewarded to bring them together. Instead of visual pleasure, women may feel the positive emotions of infatuation or affection when looking at men.

A woman will feel infatuation, for example, if she sees a man with an erect penis – but only if she caused his erection. If another woman did, she will not feel infatuation. A woman only feels infatuation when she concludes that a man is sexually attracted to her.

Women prefer muscular, tall or good-looking men because of infatuation, not visual pleasure. Muscular, tall or good-looking men are higher-rank and therefore make women feel stronger infatuation.

A woman will feel affection, for example, if she sees a man's bum. Everybody feels affection when they see features that separate humans from other primates – like white eyes, smiling and tailless bums. Tailless bums separate us from monkeys in particular.

Chapter 28
Pleasing Scenery

You feel pleasing scenery when you see lush scenery.

You feel a positive sensation when you see landscapes of trees, vegetation, water and open spaces. That sensation is called pleasing scenery in this book.

Pleasing scenery is relatively weak.

Pleasing scenery is weak compared to emotions like pride or love. However, its influence is evident in the prices paid for real estate with park views or the trouble we go to grow plants indoors.

Pleasing scenery is an easy source of happiness.

Besides cute, pleasing scenery is the only positive effect that does not have any major drawbacks. Affection requires coordination with other people. Love and infatuation do not last. Pride requires increasing your rank. Humor requires new stories. Sexual pleasure requires partners and risk. Excitement requires finding new scenery. Pleasing tastes can lead to obesity.

Pleasing scenery does not require people, work or risk – you just need scenery. And it lasts indefinitely – as long as you look at it, you feel it.

Pleasing scenery can make a significant contribution to happiness.

By itself, pleasing scenery will not make you satisfactorily happy. However, it can make a significant contribution if you actively seek it. You can, for example, make a point of living or exercising near lush scenery. You can seek careers or companies that provide daily viewing of lush scenery.

Pleasing scenery can be useful for dieters.

Enjoying pleasing scenery is a good way to replace pleasing taste or offset hunger. Instead of having dessert, go for a walk in the park.

Chapter 29
Excitement

You feel excitement when you see novel scenery.
People use the word excitement to describe two different feelings. First, they feel excitement when they're looking forward to a future event, like a party. Second, they feel excitement when they see novel scenery, like a new city.

When people are excited about a future event, they're looking forward to feeling the emotion associated with the event. In the case of a party, they're looking forward to feeling affection while being with friends. Being excited about a future event is best understood by focussing on the emotion associated with the event.

This book will only use the second meaning of excitement – the positive sensation you feel when you see novel scenery. The urge we all have to see what's around the corner or over the hill is the urge to feel excitement. What's around the corner or over the hill is novel scenery.

pleasing scenery	excitement
lush scenery	novel scenery

Pleasing scenery and excitement are different sensations.
Pleasing scenery and excitement are both positive sensations you feel when you look at scenery, however they are caused by different scenery. You feel pleasing scenery when you see lush scenery. You feel excitement when you see novel scenery.

You only feel pleasing scenery when you see a familiar forest. You only feel excitement when you see an unfamiliar desert. You feel both when you see an unfamiliar forest.

Excitement is relatively weak.

Excitement is weak compared to other positive emotions like love or pride. However, there are moments you can detect it or its absence.

You feel the strongest excitement when you first travel to new countries or new cities. You also feel weaker versions when the seasons change and you see the leaves turn color or the first snow fall. And you feel weak excitement when you first look at glossy magazines packed with photography.

You can also sense the absence of excitement the second time you see something. The second time you visit a city is not as enjoyable as the first time. The second snowfall of the winter is not as enjoyable as the first snowfall. Glossy magazines are not nearly as much fun to flip through the second time.

Excitement can lead to bad vacation and real estate decisions.

You'll feel excitement the first time you visit a vacation destination or tour a house. You won't feel that excitement on an ongoing basis, but many people fail to consider this when deciding how much they like a vacation destination or house. Then, they're disappointed when they don't enjoy a vacation destination as much the second time. Or they're disappointed they don't enjoy looking out the windows of their new home as much as they expected to.

Ideally, you could separate the effect of excitement to judge how much you will enjoy a vacation destination or a house on an ongoing basis. For real estate decisions, you can partially achieve this by taking numerous house tours to remove its novelty. It's hard to do the same for vacation destinations. All you can do is remember that destinations are rarely as much fun the second time. If you always visit new locations, you'll always feel excitement when you travel.

You feel boredom when you don't see novel scenery.

People use boredom to describe a lack of <u>any</u> stimulation. This book uses boredom to describe a specific lack of stimulation – the lack of novel scenery. When you don't see enough novel scenery, you feel the negative mental effect of boredom.

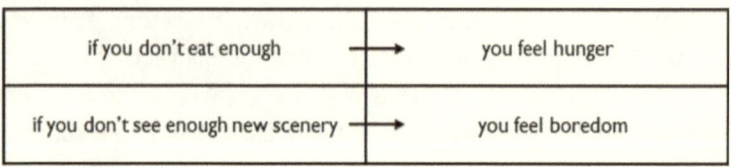

if you don't eat enough	→	you feel hunger
if you don't see enough new scenery	→	you feel boredom

Boredom works like hunger.

If you don't eat enough, you start to feel hunger. And the longer it's been since you've eaten, the stronger hunger becomes. Similarly, if you don't see enough novel scenery, you start to feel boredom. And the longer it's been since you've seen novel scenery, the stronger boredom becomes.

Boredom is relatively weak.

Boredom is so weak compared to other emotions that it's hard to detect and mentally isolate from other emotions. You might be able to detect it when it's very strong or to detect its absence after it has recently been very strong.

Boredom might be strong enough to detect if you haven't been on a trip for more than 12 months. It'll feel like a dark cloud in the background, not the stabbing pain that negative emotions like humiliation or revenge can be.

Boredom's absence might be detectable when you return from a trip. Going on a trip will stop you feeling boredom, but it will also make you feel excitement. So you can't detect boredom's absence when you're away, but you might when you return and your excitement stops. If you compare how you felt at ordinary moments before leaving with ordinary moments after you've returned, you may notice that you feel a little less depressed – that dark cloud is gone from the background. That's the absence of boredom.

Boredom should be actively managed like hunger and loneliness.
Although boredom never becomes as strong as hunger, for example, it can creep up on you and make you unhappy before you realize it. You'll feel strong boredom if you don't see novel scenery at least once a year.

It's easy to avoid boredom by ensuring that you routinely see novel scenery. At least once a year, you can vacation in a new destination. Once a quarter, you can take weekend trips to new, nearby locations. You may also be able to steer your career towards opportunities that involve travel.

Chapter 31
Pleasing Tastes

You enjoy pleasing taste when you eat.
There are four pleasing tastes: sweet, salty, fatty and umami.

Pleasing taste is a source of happiness.
Although eating seems to feel good in your mouth, the pleasing taste is really in your head – just like the emotion of love or the sensation of affection. Putting sugar on your tongue makes you feel a positive mental effect – just like seeing family does.

People may not explicitly consider pleasing taste to be a source of happiness, but they do implicitly. People routinely seek comfort foods to offset their negative emotions. And many people make eating and cooking a central part of their recreational activities.

Pleasing taste is an overused source of happiness.
The growing problem of obesity is evidence that we seek too much happiness from eating. It's not surprising. It's an immediate, positive mental effect that doesn't require much work or other people – like other positive emotions or sensations do.

And we've come to believe that we're supposed to be happy. So if we're not happy, we feel compelled to fix the problem and eating fixes the problem.

Even for those that can manage their weight, eating is overused. Fit people exercise more than necessary so they can eat more than necessary. Eventually the excess exercise results in chronic pain and early physical deterioration. The chronic pain more than offsets the happiness gained from overeating.

Dieting requires replacing pleasing taste as a source of happiness.
Dieting is more likely to succeed if another positive emotion or sensation is used to replace the loss of pleasing taste you feel when you eat less. The best candidates are pleasing scenery and affection – you can feel them on an ongoing basis. Instead of eating dessert, go for walk in the park with friends.

Overeating can be reduced by reducing food variety.
At any one meal, the pleasing taste of a food declines the more you eat it. If you stop eating a particular food for a few days, it regains its full pleasing taste when you eat it again. So we eat a variety of foods – at any one meal and over the course of a week – so that everything makes us feel the strongest pleasing taste. The more pleasing food tastes, the more we eat. The constantly growing variety of foods in our supermarkets and restaurants is contributing to our obesity problem.

If you eat the same foods every day, like dogs do, you won't enjoy eating as much. If you don't enjoy eating as much, you'll eat less. Reducing food variety may be the easiest way to lose weight.

You feel the negative mental effect of hunger if you don't eat enough.
Although you think hunger is a discomfort in your stomach, it's not. The emptiness in your stomach makes you feel a negative effect in your head. Hunger is a source of unhappiness just like loneliness or humiliation.

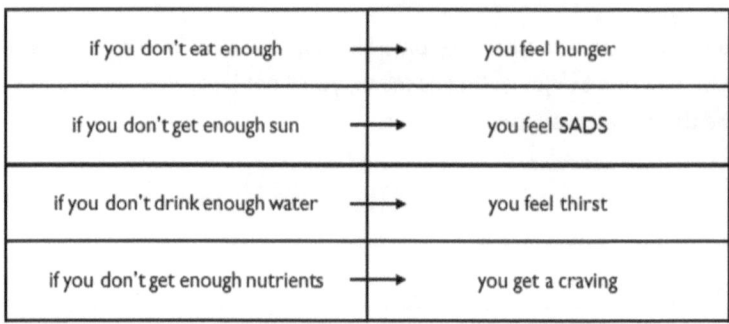

if you don't eat enough	you feel hunger
if you don't get enough sun	you feel SADS
if you don't drink enough water	you feel thirst
if you don't get enough nutrients	you get a craving

Hunger, SADS, thirst and cravings are similar.
All four are negative mental effects that you feel when you don't consume enough of an input. If you don't eat enough food, you feel hunger. If you don't get enough sunlight, you feel SADS. If you don't drink enough water, you feel thirst. If you don't get enough of a particular nutrient, you get a craving.

Loneliness, lust and boredom have a similar purpose and mental mechanism. Their negative mental effect increases until you get something you're missing.

Revenge is best managed when you're not hungry.
Revenge coerces you to retaliate against rule breakers. Resisting the urge to retaliate requires tolerating its negative mental effect. If you're also hungry, hunger's negative effect is added to revenge's negative effect. It then seems that retaliating will stop an even larger negative effect. It becomes much more difficult to resist retaliating.

You can avoid this problem by ensuring that you're not hungry in situations likely to make you feel revenge – like commuting. Try to always eat before commuting. And keep a snack in your car or briefcase.

Chapter 33
Disgust

You feel disgust when you detect a toxin.
You feel disgust, for example, when:
- you smell fecal matter
- you smell rotting flesh
- you taste rancid meat
- you taste sour milk

You do not feel disgust for other reasons.
You do not feel disgust, for example, when:
- somebody's morals disagree with yours
- somebody does something deceitful
- somebody steals from a handicapped person
- somebody does not help others

If you say somebody disgusts you for these reasons, you're trying to humiliate the other person. You're saying their rank has fallen to the level of fecal matter or rotting flesh. In other words, you're trying to lower their rank as low as possible – to maximize the humiliation they feel.

Disgust, bitter, sour and pain are similar.
All four are negative mental effects that help you avoid toxins or trauma. Disgust discourages contact with animal waste or eating toxic animal foods. Bitter discourages eating poisonous plants. Sour discourages eating rotting plants. Pain discourages activities that cause injury.

Disgust makes you frown.
You frown involuntarily when you feel disgust. You also frown involuntarily when you feel bitter, sour or pain. Frowning evolved to warn people not to eat what you just ate.

The frowning caused by disgust is momentary – you just see a quick flash. By comparison, the frowning caused by grief is sustained – you see it for a few seconds or more.

Chapter 34
Fear

You feel fear when you are threatened.
You feel fear, for example, when you:
- see a spider or a snake
- look down from a height
- see the facial expression of horror on another person
- hear a blood-curdling scream from another person
- conclude that your happiness may suddenly change

Fear's mental effect suppresses positive and negative emotions.
When you feel fear, you don't feel happy or unhappy. While frightened, you can't enjoy humor or sexual pleasure. And you can't feel humiliation or loneliness. Fear's emotional suppression focuses you on the threat.

Fear's physical effects prepare you to fight or flee.
Fear can cause the following to occur:
- adrenalin release
- heart rate increase
- palms and feet sweat
- hair stands on end
- bladder evacuation

The greater your fear, the more of this list occurs. For slight fear, adrenalin is released and your heart rate increases. For extreme fear, everything occurs including bladder evacuation.

Fear can also cause the involuntary expressions of horror and screaming.
If you're moderately frightened, you'll involuntarily make the facial expression of horror – three circles formed by wide open eyes and mouth. If you're extremely frightened, you'll also scream – a blood curdling scream.

While these expressions warn of others of danger, they don't help you. Screaming, for example, warns others about a predator, but tells a predator exactly where you are.

You feel fear when you conclude your happiness may suddenly change.
You feel fear, for example, if you're confronted by a robber. You feel fear because you conclude that you may suddenly feel pain or humiliation.

This reaction occurs for any <u>negative emotion</u>. If you see a situation unfolding that's likely to make you feel a negative emotion like revenge, you will conclude that your happiness is about to worsen which makes you feel fear. When you conclude that another driver is about to cut you off, for example, your heart rate increases.

After a situation has unfolded and you're feeling a negative emotion, your happiness stops changing and you stop feeling fear. After another driver cuts you off, for example, you feel revenge but your heart rate returns to normal.

A minute or two of elevated heart rate is common whenever you conclude that you might suddenly feel negative emotions like revenge, compassion, guilt, humiliation, envy, loneliness, grief, heartbreak or jealousy.

Surprisingly, this reaction also occurs for any <u>positive emotion</u>. If you learn that you might win an award and feel pride, for example, your heart rate will increase. After you confirm that have won and you feel pride, your heart rate returns to normal.

A minute or two of elevated heart rate is common whenever you conclude that you might suddenly feel positive emotions like pride, love, infatuation or affection.
" He's so dreamy – he makes my heart race."

Being stressed means frequently concluding your happiness may change.
If you're juggling many balls, for example, you'll frequently learn that there may be a problem with one of the balls. Every time you learn there may be a problem, you conclude that your happiness may suddenly change – which makes you feel fear and causes your heart rate to increase.

You keep feeling that fear until you resolve how big the problem is. Once you do, your fear stops because you know your happiness will not change further – until you learn of the next potential problem.

fear	worry
immediate threats	future threats
suppressive mental effect	imagined negative mental effect
increased heart rate, sweaty hands, . . .	no physical effects

Fear and worry are different.
Fear is about immediate threats. Worry is about future threats. You feel fear when a robber points a gun at you. You worry when you learn that your neighbour was robbed at gunpoint.

While fear suppresses all emotions, worry makes you imagine a negative emotion in the future. When frightened by a robber, you don't feel happy or unhappy. When worrying about being robbed, you feel unhappy because you imagine feeling pain or humiliation.

While fear makes you react physically, worry does not. When frightened by a robber, your heart rate increases. When worrying about being robbed in the future, your heart rate does not increase.

Thrill seekers and horror film audiences seek fear.
When somebody parachutes from a plane or bungee jumps, they feel fear for an extended period. During that time, they don't feel any negative emotions. While jumping, parachutists don't feel loneliness or humiliation.

Horror film audiences achieve the same outcome for longer. As audiences imagine being the victim, they vicariously feel fear. While they're on the edge of their seats, they escape their negative emotions for a few hours.

Fear is not important to happiness.
Thrill seekers and horror film audiences aside, fear's suppressive mental effect only lasts a few seconds a few times a day at most.

Chapter 35
Startle

You feel startle when you're surprised.
You feel startle, for example, when you:
- hear a loud noise
- feel yourself moving unexpectedly
- hear a quiet noise that you did not expect
- feel something make contact with you that you did not expect
- think you're alone, look up and see someone quietly standing there

Like fear, startle's mental effect suppresses positive and negative emotions.
While startled, you can't feel emotions like humor or humiliation.

Startle's physical effects make you involuntarily protect yourself.
When startled, you involuntarily:
- raise your arms to protect your neck and torso
- tense your neck and face muscles
- close your eyelids

Startle evolved to minimize the damage caused by ambush predators, like lions. You raise your arms to protect your head and torso because it's better to injure your arms than your torso. Tensing your neck and face muscles makes them less likely to tear. Closing your eyelids helps protect your eyes from scratching or gouging.

Startle is not important to happiness.
Startle's suppressive mental effect only lasts a few seconds a few times a day at most.

Chapter 36
Analyzing Happiness

1. social	affection loneliness, crying	Do you cry more than once a week?
2. primary rank	pride humiliation	Is your rank up, flat or down?
3. romantic	monogynic love infatuation	Which stage of romance are you in?
4. parental	maternal love grandmaternal love	Are you a mother or grandmother?
5. humor	humor, laughter	Do you enjoy humor >4 hrs/ wk?
6. scenic	pleasing scenery excitement, boredom	Do you see lush scenery daily? Do you see new scenery annually?
7. sexual	sexual pleasure lust	Do you consider sex important?
8. eating	pleasing taste hunger	Are you overweight?
9. hazards	envy revenge, anger compassion, selfish guilt	Do you feel envy most days? Do you get angry most days? Do you feel sorry for others most days?

This chart provides a checklist and questions to analyze your happiness.
Emotions with common or connected causes are grouped together. And they are listed in order of priority – those at the top are most important.

The first four groups are the major emotions: social, primary rank, romantic and parental. They are much stronger than the groups that follow. Your happiness is largely determined by what happens in these groups.

The next four groups are the minor emotions: humor, scenic, sexual and eating. These groups can be good sources of happiness, but never to the degree that the major emotions can. The last group are hazards, which only reduce happiness and should be avoided.

1. Getting enough affection to avoid loneliness is the first priority.
Affection is the best source of happiness. The affection you feel when you see old friends or family can be strong - almost as strong as the other major positive emotions of pride, love and infatuation. More importantly, it's permanent and the other major positive emotions are not. You can keep feeling affection from a friend or family member forever. Pride, love and infatuation are all temporary. You stop feeling pride when your higher rank is no longer new. Men stop feeling love for a woman 46 months after meeting her. Women stop feeling infatuation for a man after 8 months. Mothers and grandmothers stop feeling love when a child or grandchild is 33 months old.

If you don't get enough affection, you feel lonely – the most common source of unhappiness. Long ago, we felt strong affection all day every day. We spent most of our waking hours interacting with very familiar people. Now we spend a small fraction of our days with people that are very familiar. We spend most of our time with people that are relatively unfamiliar or complete strangers. Although we're interacting with people all day long, they're making us feel little or no affection. As a result, most people are lonely.

It's hard to mentally detect and isolate loneliness. It never causes you to feel the obvious mental discomfort that negative emotions like revenge or humiliation can. Instead, it just puts you in a constantly down mood. And you become so accustomed to it that you think it's normal. Occasionally, you get enough affection to stop the loneliness. During those brief periods, you think you feel happy. However, you don't feel happy – you just stopped feeling unhappy. You briefly stopped feeling loneliness.

There are two ways to tell if you're getting enough affection to avoid loneliness:
- hours per week you spend with familiar people
- number of times per week you cry

How many hours per week do you spend with familiar people? Add up the hours you spend with people you've known for five or more years. Obviously this includes family and friends. It may also include co-workers. Only add hours that involve direct interaction. So having dinner or a meeting counts, but watching a movie or sporting event does not.

Long ago, we spent at least 10-12 hours a day or ~75 hours a week with familiar people. It's unknown how many hours we need to spend with familiar people to avoid loneliness. However, it must be at least a third of the 75 hours we spent together in the past – which means at least 25 hours a week.

If you spend less than 25 hours a week with familiar people, you're probably lonely. However, this is just a crude indicator that you're lonely.

Crying is a solid indicator that you're lonely. Although loneliness is hard to detect, crying is not and you only cry if you're lonely. Many other emotions can cause you to release suppressed crying, but only one emotion is the root cause of crying before it is suppressed – loneliness.

Do you cry more than once a week? If you do, you're lonely. The crying doesn't have to be a full blown balling session. You're lonely even if you just shed a tear or suppress the urge to cry. A good time to assess crying is when you're watching a tear-jerker movie. If you cry while watching a movie that makes you feel strong emotions, you're lonely. Most people do.

If cry more than once a week, you should increase the amount of affection you get until you cry less than once a week.

There are five ways to increase the amount of affection you get.

First, you could interact with more people that are familiar. You could, for example, arrange to meet on a weekly basis with a friend or family member you don't normally interact with.

Second, you could spend more time per person with the familiar people you already interact with. Each week, you could spend another night out with friends or another weekend afternoon with family members.

Third, you could shift your time to more familiar people. You could spend less time with casual friends and more time with your best friends or family.

Fourth, you could be more intimate with people. Instead of seeing a movie with old friends, for example, you could have dinner facing each other.

Fifth, you could spend more time with alternatives to real people. Instead of exercising alone, for example, you could get a dog and walk it twice a day.

In addition to getting enough affection week-to-week, it's good to think about year-to-year changes. If you lose an important source of affection, for example, you should replace the loss. You should find replacements whenever relationships end, friends move or somebody dies.

An important part of year-to-year planning are long-term sources of affection. The relative importance of affection grows as you age and other emotions, like the romantic emotions, become less important. And you feel the strongest affection from your most familiar family and friends – your long-term sources of affection.

It generally believed that you should look to family for long-term sources of affection – your siblings in particular. However, friends are better long-term sources of affection. They can make you feel affection nearly as strong as siblings can, but they try harder and don't make you feel envy.

2. Pride and humiliation are the second priority.
Pride and humiliation are the strongest emotions you feel throughout your life. Love and infatuation can be equally strong, but they're only active for the middle third of your life and only for durations of 33, 42 or 8 months.

While affection provides the baseline of your happiness, pride and humiliation are the peaks and valleys of happiness. Many of your happiest memories will moments of extreme pride. Many of your unhappiest memories will moments of extreme humiliation.

To understand how pride and humiliation are affecting your happiness, you need to understand how your rank is changing. If your rank has gone up, you feel pride. If you expect your rank to go up, you imagine feeling pride. If your rank has gone down, you feel humiliation. If you expect your rank to go down, you imagine feeling humiliation.

Don't worry about day-to-day changes in your rank even though they will make you feel pride and humiliation. While day-to-day changes are important, that's not the best timeframe to begin your analysis.

The best timeframe is two years – backwards and forwards. You rarely feel pride or humiliation from events that happened more than two years ago. And you rarely feel imagined pride or humiliation from events that are more than two years in the future.

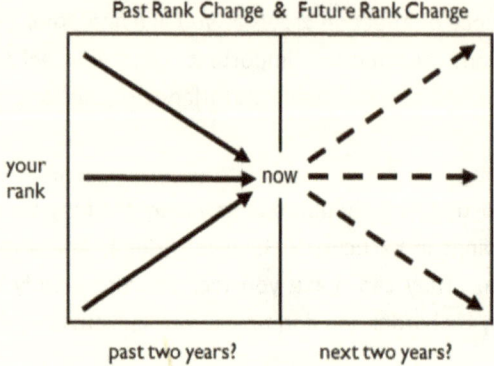

Past Rank Change & Future Rank Change

<u>During the past two years, is your rank up, flat or down?</u>
<u>During the next two years, do you expect your rank to be up, flat or down?</u>

Your answers will put you into one of nine situations:
- Up & Up — the happiest situation
- Up & Flat — tied for second happiest
- Up & Down — top of the roller coaster
- Flat & Up — tied for second happiest
- Flat & Flat — the middle of the happiness spectrum
- Flat & Down — tied for second unhappiest
- Down & Up — the bottom of the roller coaster
- Down & Flat — tied for second unhappiest
- Down & Down — the unhappiest situation

Your happiness is largely determined by which of these situations you fall into. Each situation is reviewed on the pages that follow.

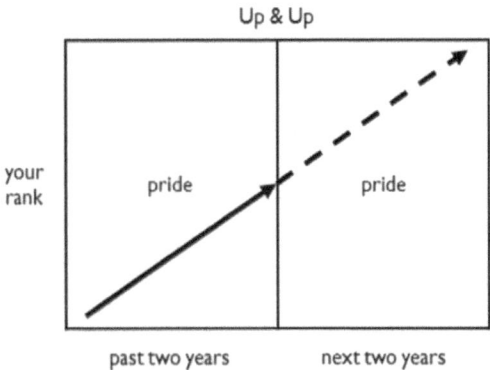

Up & Up

your rank   pride   pride

past two years   next two years

2a. Up & Up: the happiest situation.

Your rank has gone during the past two years and you expect it to continue going up during the next two. You've recently been promoted at work, for example, and expect to be promoted again in the future. The past and the future make you feel pride.

This is the ideal situation.   You are maximizing pride and minimizing humiliation. To maintain this situation, you must always be thinking about increasing your rank.   Put simply, always being ambitious will make you happiest.

The best employers and video game makers know this is the happiest situation. The best employers give good employees a constant stream of promotions to make them feel continuous pride.   The best video games constantly move players to higher levels or ranking to make them feel continuous pride.

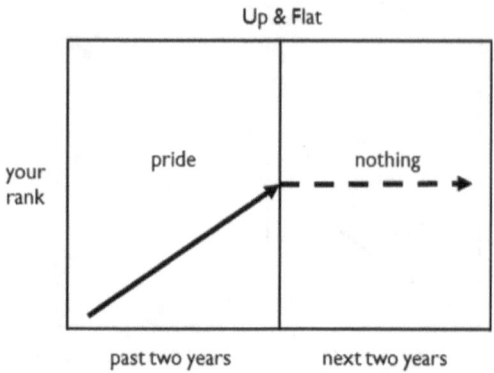

Up & Flat

your rank

pride   nothing

past two years   next two years

2b. Up & Flat: tied for second happiest.

Your rank has gone up during the past two years, but you expect it to be flat during the next two. You've recently been promoted at work, for example, but don't expect another promotion in the future. The past makes you feel pride, but the future makes you feel nothing.

While you are currently happy, you won't be in the future when pride ends. If nothing changes, your situation will become a Flat & Flat – an unstable situation which often leads to a mid-life crisis or worse.

This situation is avoided by being more ambitious. If your current employer does not offer opportunities, look at new employers. If your career does not offer opportunities, look at new hobbies or recreational activities. Just thinking about whether you could succeed in these alternatives will make you feel imagined pride.

Up & Down

your rank | pride | humiliation

past two years | next two years

2c. Up & Down: top of the roller coaster.

Your rank has gone up during the past two years, but you expect it to go down during the next two. You've recently been promoted at work, for example, but expect to fail in your new position. You feel mixed happiness. The past makes you feel pride, but the future makes you feel humiliation.

This situation can be a normal part of the game of life or a watershed moment that leads to a disastrous Down & Down situation. It depends on the reason you expect your rank to fall.

If you expect your rank to fall because you overreached with your ambition, you should do nothing but continue to be ambitious. If you can't fix the problem with your new position, for example, you should move to a position you can succeed at. You want to get back to an Up & Up situation.

If you expect your rank to fall for reasons other than overreaching, you need to change something. If family or romance are intruding on your career, for example, you should change them before your work rank falls. Without a good source of income, who cares about family or romance. And it's easier to prevent a decline than to reverse it. You're trying to arrest or avoid your decline and get to a Flat & Flat situation.

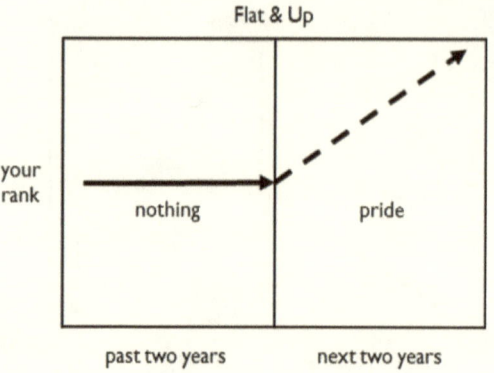

Flat & Up

past two years | next two years

your rank — nothing — pride

2d. Flat & Up: tied for second happiest.
Your rank has been flat during the past two years, but you expect it to go up during the next two. You haven't been promoted recently, for example, but are expecting a promotion or new job in the future. Although the past makes you feel nothing, the future makes you feel pride.

This is a good place to be. Ideally, your rank will go up and make your situation become an Up & Up.

This situation applies to lottery ticket buyers. Their past rank is usually flat, but they can credibly imagine their rank going up because they have a ticket. Even if they don't win, buying a ticket allows them to imagine pride until the draw.

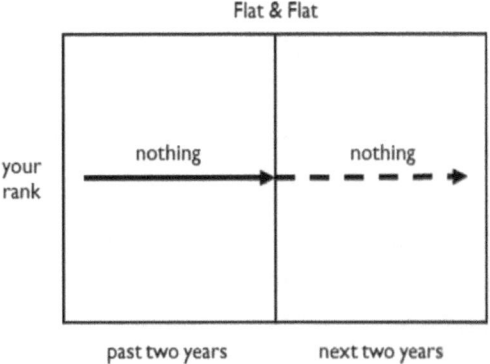

Flat & Flat

your rank

nothing　　　　nothing

past two years　　　next two years

2e. Flat & Flat: the middle of the happiness spectrum.

Your rank has been flat during the past two years and you expect it to stay flat in the future. You haven't been promoted recently, for example, and don't expect to be in the future. The past and the future make you feel nothing.

The very young and very old fall are in this situation. The very young don't feel rank emotions until they are two. The very old are more focussed on surviving.

People feeling love or infatuation also fall into this category. People feeling these emotions are more focussed on others than their rank.

For everybody else, this a bad place to be. It's unhappy and unstable.

Most people in this situation are in a mid-life crisis. Their rank rose constantly in their early years, making them feel constant pride. Now at mid-life, their rank has been flat for years. The loss of constant pride feels like depression. People in this situation should find ways to increase their rank and feel pride.

Instead, people in a mid-life crisis often seek happiness in other emotions. Some seek more romance which means finding a new partner. Some women have children to feel maternal love. Others may seek happiness in sexual pleasure. Most commonly, people replace lost pride with pleasing taste – they eat more.

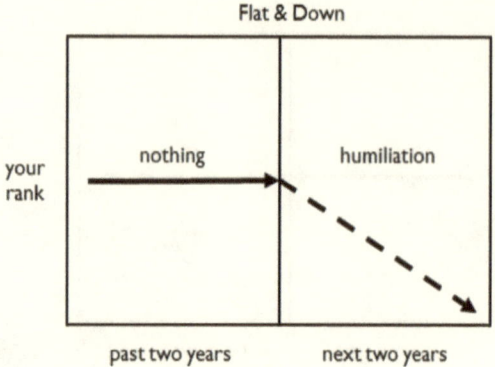

Flat & Down

your rank — nothing — humiliation

past two years — next two years

2f. Flat & Down: tied for second unhappiest.

Your rank has been flat during the past two years, but you expect it to go down during the next two. You haven't been promoted recently, for example, and expect that you may be fired in the future. The past makes you feel nothing and the future makes you feel humiliation.

This is tied for the second unhappiest situation. You can't feel good about anything and there is reason to worry that things will worsen.

The best thing is to address the threat to your rank. Assuming you can't prevent the decline, then it may be best to make the future unfold now. Like ripping a bandage off, the sooner your rank goes down, the sooner you'll start and then stop feeling humiliation. And you'll immediately stop imagining humiliation in the future.

With humiliation out of the way, you can then return to finding ways to increase your rank and feel pride again. Or not. You could just enjoy the absence of humiliation. Either way, you'll be happier than you are now.

Down & Up

your
rank   humiliation   pride

past two years   next two years

2g. Down & Up: bottom of the roller coaster.

Your rank has gone down during the past two years, but you expect it to go up during the next two. You've recently been fired, for example, but have good prospects for a new job. You feel mixed happiness. Although the past makes you feel humiliation, the future makes you feel pride.

Like Up & Down, this situation is a normal part of the game of life. You fail, you pick yourself up and you try again. The humiliation you feel from past failures is offset by pride you imagine feeling in the future.

Key to staying motivated in this situation is remembering that the humiliation you currently feel will stop. And then you'll just feel imagined pride until it becomes real pride in the future.

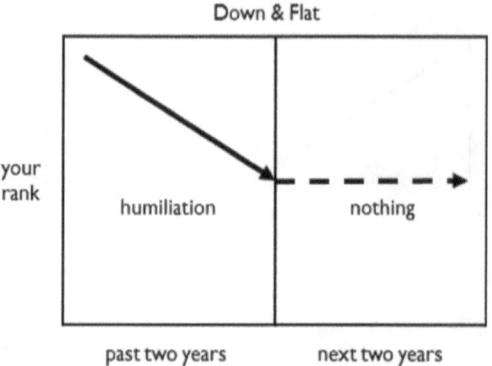

Down & Flat

your rank

humiliation

nothing

past two years

next two years

2h. Down & Flat: tied for second unhappiest.

Your rank has gone down during the past two years, but you expect it to be flat during the next two. You've recently been fired, for example, and have no good prospects for a new job, but do have ample savings. Or you've recently retired from work. The past makes you feel humiliation and the future makes you feel nothing. You're not happy and have no reason to be.

This is not a good situation, but it can become much worse if you mistakenly assume the humiliation you're feeling is permanent. Faced with the prospect of feeling humiliation forever, you'll be tempted to mask your humiliation with food, alcohol or drugs. That will lead to a permanent addiction that will continue after humiliation ends. Your situation could worsen to a Down & Down. Instead of masking the humiliation, it's best to just live with the it – it won't last for more than a year. And look for opportunities to increase your rank and change your situation to Down & Up.

When retirement from work causes this scenario, there is an added problem. The retirement also causes a loss of affection that can be more harmful to happiness than humiliation – particularly if you spent many years with former co-workers. That loss of affection will make you lonely. The humiliation will eventually stop – as discussed above. But the loneliness will just worsen – unless you take steps to replace the lost affection.

Down & Down

your rank | humiliation | humiliation

past two years | next two years

2i. Down & Down: the unhappiest situation.

Your rank has gone down during the past two years and you expect it to go down during the next two. You've recently been fired, for example, and have no good prospects for a new job and no savings. The past makes you feel humiliation and the future makes you feel humiliation.

This is the worst situation to be in. Correcting it is a very high priority.

Like ripping a bandage off, it may be better to get to the low rank you expect to fall to – the sooner you reach your bottom, the sooner you stop feeling humiliation and the sooner you can begin to imagine pride.

If you're a homeowner, for example, you should consider selling your home before you have to. Yes, you won't be homeowner anymore. But, you'll stop feeling humiliation. That will allow you to start imagining better days and feeling imagined pride. You will move to Flat & Flat and then Flat & Up.

Assuming that you're getting enough affection, correcting this situation should be your first priority. It's the easiest way to improve your happiness.

3. Romance has four stages.

Although love and infatuation are among the strongest positive emotions, they are only the third priority. While you feel affection and pride continually throughout your life, you only feel the romantic emotions while you're in love. Men only love a woman for 42 months and most men only fall in love with 2-4 women during their lifetimes. Women are only infatuated with a man for 8 months and most women only become strongly infatuated with 4-8 men during their lifetimes.

Romantic emotions are not a mystery. You know from this book, for instance, that everybody is programmed to fall out of love and move on to a new partner. You can use these insights to navigate through the romantic emotions – enjoying them with minimal effort and avoiding their drawbacks.

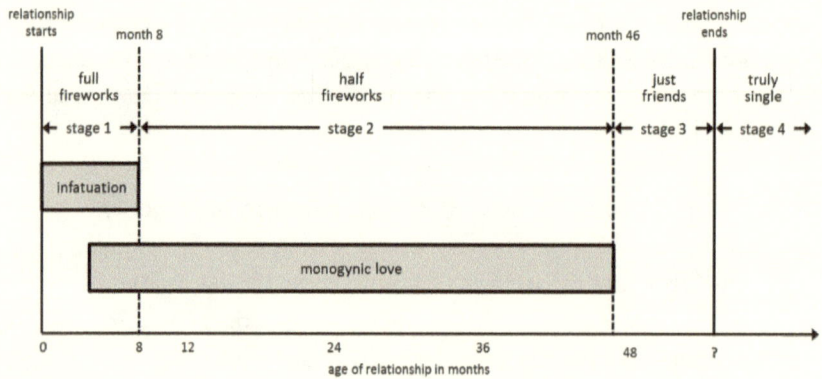

Childless romantic relationships have four stages:

- 0-8 months   stage 1: full fireworks
- 8-46 months   stage 2: half fireworks
- > 46 months and together   stage 3: just friends
- > 46 months and apart   stage 4: truly single

Which of the four romantic stages are you currently in? Said another way, how many months have passed since you last started dating somebody?

All couples move through these stages on the same timing. If you know your stage, then you know what each partner currently feels, when this stage ends and what each partner will feel next – as described on the following pages.

128

3a. Stage 1: full fireworks – both partners feel strong positive emotions.

The stage occurs from month 0 to 8 of a relationship. During this stage both partners feel very strong positive emotions – but not the same emotions or motivations. Men feel monogynic love which motivates men to make their woman happy. Women feel infatuation which motivates them to attract the sexual interest of the man. While men spend money buying presents for their women, women spend money on themselves to be more attractive.

In addition to feeling infatuation, women's sexual pleasure is elevated during the second 4 months of this stage. During this short window, women enjoy sex almost as much as men do. So both partners are happy and horny.

At any given time, only a tiny percentage of couples are in stage 1. It's easy to spot couples who are. They're the ones who "should get a room".

3b. Stage 2: half fireworks – only men feel a strong positive emotion.

This stage occurs from month 8 to 46 of a relationship. This is the 38 month gap during which men continue to feel fireworks, but women do not.

While men continue to feel monogynic love throughout this stage, women stop feeling infatuation. And women's sexual pleasure is no longer elevated. They are not happy or horny. The only positive emotion women feel from their man is affection – which is weak because the relationship is so new. Without infatuation, women are no longer motivated to attract the man's sexual interest – just his presence, which is all they need to feel affection.

The sudden loss of infatuation leaves women feeling unhappy – when they're supposed to be happy. Women try to replace this loss with happiness from alternatives. Some work harder to feel pride at work. Others seek pride by getting engaged, married or pregnant. Some seek infatuation from other men.

If women seek infatuation from other men, by flirting for example, their men will feel jealousy since they still feel monogynic love. By contrast, women won't feel heartbreak if their man cheats since they no longer feel infatuation.

For both partners, this stage is a mixed blessing. Men feel monogynic love, but their woman is not content and may move on to another man. Women are not happy, but they do have a man who is happy to be their slave for a few years.

At any given time, only a small percentage of couples are in this stage. Couples in this stage are happy to be together, but you can tell they're no longer couples who "should get a room". And it's probably evident that the man is content, but the woman is not. She talks about the future more than he does.

3c. Stage 3: just friends – both partners only feel affection.
This stage occurs after month 46 of a relationship. The vast majority of couples are in this stage. Neither partner feels fireworks. Women stopped feeling infatuation back at month 8. And men have stopped feeling monogynic love at month 46. Both partners only feel the weaker emotion of affection – which is mistakenly thought to be a weaker form of love.

In addition to losing monogynic love, men only feel weak visual pleasure when looking at their woman. But men still feel strong visual pleasure when looking at novel women.

At this stage, neither partner is motivated to please the other partner. They are only motivated by affection to be with the other person – whether the other person is pleased or not. However, that affection prevents them feeling loneliness. Even couples who constantly fight are making each other feel affection and are therefore avoiding loneliness.

It's important to recognize that all romantic relationships reach this stage and on this timing – regardless of who is involved or what they do. Nobody should think that somebody failed when a relationship reaches this stage and cools.

This stage is the least stable. Both partners want to feel romantic emotions again. However, they can never feel fireworks again with their current partner – only with a stranger. Adding to the instability is the mistaken assumption that fireworks can last forever if you find the right person.

If a couple stays together, the affection they feel will gradually grow stronger the more time they spend together. After a few decades that affection can grow as strong as weak love or infatuation.

Couples should not consider marriage until year 5 of a relationship. At that point, neither partner has been influenced by fireworks for at least a year. There's no reason to expect either person's behavior to change in the future. And there's no reason to expect perceptions of the other person to change. If you still like the other person at this stage, you'll probably still like them decades from now. Since your spouse will probably be your most important long-term source of affection, it's worth waiting to get this decision right.

3d. Stage 4: truly single – just less affection
This stage occurs when a relationship ends after more than 46 months. Not much changes. Since all fireworks were done by month 46, both partners only felt affection from each other at the time of their break-up. That affection was moderately strong after more than 46 months. Since they won't be together, they'll make each other feel less affection. If that lost affection is not replaced by interaction with other familiar people, they'll feel more loneliness.

The obvious upside to being single is the opportunity to meet another stranger and ride the romance roller coaster.

The obvious downside is less affection and more loneliness. The more time you spend with strangers, the less time you spend with familiar people who make you feel strong affection. The less affection you feel, the more lonely you are.

A less obvious downside is <u>weaker affection in the future</u>. Affection grows stronger the more time you spend with someone. If you stick with one person and do not ride the romance roller coaster, you'll maximize the affection your partner makes you feel. If you ride the roller coaster, the partner you settle down with at the end of your romantic life will have spent much less time with you. They'll make you feel weaker affection than you could feel if you'd stuck with one person.

4. Parental emotions only apply to mothers and grandmothers.
The parental emotions don't apply directly to men. Fathers and grandfathers don't feel love for their children or grandchildren. They do feel cute – which everybody feels when they see an infant. Fathers and grandfathers also feel affection when they see or hear their children and grandchildren, but they feel this from anybody who is familiar.

Are you a mother or grandmother? Are your children or grandchildren less than 33 months old? Mothers and grandmothers with children or grandchildren less than 33 months old are very happy people – they feel maternal or grandmaternal love.

Once a child is 33 months old, in the terrible-two's, mothers stop feeling love. They only feel the weaker emotion of affection from their child, which doesn't motivate mothers to make their child happy. The also applies to grandmothers and their grandchildren.

Mothers and grandmothers should expect the end of love at 33 months. It'll feel like depression. Knowing to expect this emotional decline should help mothers and grandmothers avoid mistakenly blaming the decline on another cause or trying a solution that does not address the problem – like therapeutic or pharmaceutical help.

The end of maternal love means women can feel infatuation again. Infatuation is temporarily suppressed while women feel maternal love.

Parental emotions can affect men indirectly. Men will receive less attention from wives while they feel maternal or grandmaternal love. And they should expect their wives to become unhappy when the love stops after 33 months.

5. Humor is an easy way to be happy.

Although humor is not as strong as love or pride, it has few drawbacks. It doesn't require courtship or childcare, like love. It doesn't require the hard work required increase your rank, like pride. And it's not accompanied by downside risks, like the potential grief and humiliation that accompanies love and pride. Humor is like dessert that doesn't make you fat.

Humor's one drawback is that it's one-time. Once you hear a joke, for example, it's no longer funny. You need to keep finding new material to keep feeling humor.

Excluding gossip, do you enjoy at least 4 hours of humor a week? Since humor is an easy-to-feel, moderately strong positive emotion, it would be foolish to not ensure that you are regularly enjoying it. And you can combine trips for humor with friends or family to also get affection.

Gossip is not recommended as a source of humor because it leads to trouble. You have to provide gossip to hear it. And others will learn what you have said about them and retaliate. It's hard to resist the urge to gossip, but resisting it will make you happier in the long run. And you'll have more friends.

Do you seek humor focused on mistakes that you could make? The more likely you are to make a mistake described in a joke or portrayed in a comedy, the stronger the humor you'll feel. If you're clumsy, for example, you'll enjoy the humor of The Three Stooges. If you're not clumsy, you won't.

6. Scenic sensations are an overlooked source of happiness.

The scenic sensations are caused by scenery. You feel pleasing scenery when you see lush scenery. You feel excitement when you see novel scenery.

Like humor, scenic sensations are an appealing source of happiness. They can also be moderately strong, particularly if you see scenery that is both lush and novel – making you feel both pleasing scenery and excitement. And they're easy to feel – you just need to look at scenery. Although excitement requires finding new scenery like finding new jokes, you can feel pleasing scenery forever by looking at the same lush scenery.

Surprisingly, scenic sensations are a higher priority than sexual or eating sensations – which are stronger than scenic sensations. Although scenic sensations are weaker, they are continuous – sexual and eating sensations are not. You can enjoy a scene continuously. You can only enjoy sex or eating for a 5-15 minutes per session. And scenic sensations don't have any downside, like sexual and eating sensations. Too much sex can lead to injury or infection. Too much eating can lead to obesity. You can't look at too much scenery.

Scenic sensations are also a higher priority because they need emphasis. Sexual and eating sensations do not. Most people do not realize how much scenery can contribute to happiness. As a result, most people don't seek as much happiness from scenery as they could. By contrast, everybody realizes how much the sexual and eating sensations can contribute to happiness.

Do you see lush scenery daily? Seeing lush scenery daily is an easy way to boost your happiness. You can add lush scenery to your daily routine at home, at work, when commuting or exercising. If you make it a priority, you can pick homes that face parks, work at companies in the suburbs, commute along parkways or jog through forests. Seeing lush scenery everyday will make a significant contribution to the baseline of your happiness.

Do you see new scenery at least once a year? If you see new scenery at least once a year, you will feel excitement and you won't feel boredom. It's easy to do this by always traveling to new locations whenever you take a vacation.

7. Sexual pleasure is an overused source of happiness.
Sexual pleasure is not important to happiness. Although sex can be very pleasurable, it only lasts 5-15 minutes a session – a small percentage of total happiness.

Despite this, many people consider sex to be important to happiness. They believe you can't be happy if you're not having good sex. In reality, your happiness has little do with sex. You can have great sex and be very unhappy. And you can have bad sex and be very happy.

The overuse of sex is driven by the belief that we're supposed to be happy. If you're not happy, you're failing. To correct this supposed failure, people overuse sources of happiness that provide quick and reliable happiness – shopping, eating and sex. These solutions make you feel happy in the short term, but less happy long term.

Do you consider sex important to happiness? If you do, you could be happier by seeking more happiness elsewhere – specifically, the major emotions. You would be happier if you paid more to feeling affection or pride, for example.

Instead of thinking about how you can make a few minutes of sex feel better, you could try being a better conversationalist. Your enjoyment of sex will not change – it will still be very pleasurable for a few moments. But you'll feel more affection and pride as more friends want to hear what you have to say.

The sexual sensations of the two genders differ as much as their genitalia. People believe the other sex feels the same sexual sensations as they do. This mistaken assumption often leads to unnecessary trouble in relationships. That trouble can be avoided by remembering the differences described below.

Men should remember that women don't feel visual pleasure. What turns men on visually doesn't turn women on – like strip teases or exhibitionism.

Women should remember that the visual pleasure men feel looking at a woman declines with her novelty. Men grow steadily less interested in looking a woman – regardless of what she looks like or does. However, they remain interested in looking at novel women.

Men should remember that women do not feel lust. Women will want less sex and for biological reasons – not because the woman is frigid.

Women should remember that men do feel lust. Men need regular sex to avoid the discomfort of lust – not because they are sexually greedy.

People falling in love should remember that <u>women's vaginal pleasure is only temporarily elevated</u> during months 4-8 of a relationship. If both partners know it's temporary, nobody will wonder if there's a problem when it ends. They'll know it's a normal change that occurs when a relationship moves from stage 1 to stage 2 of romance. And both partners can adjust accordingly. Men will know to expect something less than sex all the time. Women will feel okay turning the tempo down knowing that men understand.

Men should remember that <u>women do not feel vaginal orgasm – just clitoral</u>. While men have orgasms from intercourse, women typically do not. They only have orgasm from clitoral stimulation. Assuming vaginal pleasure is not temporarily elevated, sexual intercourse is a chore for women. Men can change this by realizing that clitoral orgasm is the equivalent to penile orgasm. If men want sex to be satisfying for women, men need to focus on the clitoris.

8. Eating is also an overused source of happiness.
<u>Are you overweight?</u> If you're overweight, you're probably overusing eating or pleasing taste as a source of happiness.

Because eating is such an easy way to make yourself happy, it's usually people's first choice on the happiness menu. Eating tasty food immediately masks any negative emotions. You don't feel loneliness or humiliation when you put ice cream on your tongue.

The belief that we're supposed to be happy has also contributed to overeating. People believe we're supposed to be happy. If they're not happy, they're failing. So they fix the failure by eating.

Our currently archaic understanding of emotions is the root of the problem. We fully understand our physical organs, like the heart or liver, but almost nothing about our mental organs, like love or envy. This book solves this problem by making it easy for everyone to understand what emotions are.

One of the revelations from this book is that we aren't supposed to be happy. Emotions are carrots and sticks that motivate us to do what is best for our species. On average, you feel carrots and sticks in equal measure. You feel pride, for example, when your rank goes up. And you feel humiliation when your rank goes down. You will naturally be happy and unhappy. You're not failing if you're unhappy. However, unless you actively navigate away from negative emotions and towards positive emotions, you will be less happy than you could be.

Dieting, for example, is not about managing your weight or calories. Dieting is about managing your happiness by replacing pleasing taste with an alternative positive emotion or sensation – such as humor or pleasing scenery. You can use this book like a menu to find which alternative suits you best.

9. Hazards are to be avoided.
Everybody thinks about improving their happiness by feeling more positive emotions. These opportunities are well explored – spend more time with family to feel affection, work harder to increase your rank to feel pride, find a romantic partner to feel love or infatuation.

By contrast, few people think about improving their happiness by avoiding negative emotions. Because it's less explored, avoiding negative emotions may offer more potential to improve happiness.

Hazards are negative emotions that can be avoided – envy, revenge, compassion. By comparison, grief and humiliation are negative emotions that can't be avoided. You must risk feeling them if you want to feel love or pride.

In addition to improving your happiness, avoiding hazards also avoids legal trouble and physical injury. Hazard emotions encourage you to harm yourself to help the greater good.

The easiest way to avoid hazards is to avoid the situations or people that cause them. And for those situations and people you can't avoid, it's best to develop the habit of doing nothing.

Do you feel envy most days?

Envy is best avoided by avoiding peers that have excelled. That usually means avoiding siblings or friends. Instead, socialize with people who are your rank.

For envy that you can't avoid, don't do anything. Just learn to live with it. You could work hard to catch-up to someone you envy. And when your rank equals their rank, you'll stop feeling envy – towards that person. You'll still envy other people. You'll never escape it entirely. Instead of working extra hard to close the rank gap, seek positive emotions – enjoy affection and humor with friends.

Do you get angry most days?

If you frequently get angry, you frequently feel revenge. Revenge is best avoided by avoiding situations likely to involve rule breakers – like rush hour commuting. Instead of commuting at rush hour, go earlier or later. Or change your career to work from home or move to the city.

Where you cannot avoid rule breakers, it's best to develop the habit of doing and saying nothing. Given how strong revenge can be, it's necessary to not even picture how you would retaliate. If you do picture retaliating, you'll act on impulse the next time you feel a surge of revenge. Instead, put your effort into finding a way to avoid the rule breakers in the first place. Don't park near the entrances to stores – park in the corner where nobody will bug you.

Let other victims punish rule breakers for the benefit of all. Road ragers do serve a purpose – there would be more jerks on the road if some drivers didn't rage against them.

Do you feel sorry for others most days?

Compassion is best avoided by avoiding situations that are likely to make you feel compassion – like streets lined with panhandlers. Avoiding these situations also avoids feeling selfish guilt afterwards. If you're not aware of misfortune, you can't feel selfish guilt for not helping.

Index

erectile dysfunction   56
excitement   12, 101-4, 133
eye contact   7, 23-24
eye-for-eye retaliation   18, 62
exercising   37, 46, 101, 117, 134
exhibitionism   135

fat jokes   55
fathers   8, 10, 20, 63, 77-78, 83-84, 86-87, 97, 132
fear   57, 110-110
feet   84, 110
fellatio   18
female sexual pleasure   99
fireworks   15, 25, 128-131, 136
first-time offenders   41
flirting   18, 20, 129
food variety   107
forgiving   62
friends   6, 11, 26-27, 31, 35-36, 40, 47, 51, 58-59, 73, 75, 77-78, 81, 86, 88,
        102, 106, 115-17, 128, 130, 133, 135, 138
frowning   87, 109
funny   12, 53-59, 133

g-spot   99
gay   17, 57, 95
gossip   27, 53-58, 85, 133
grandchildren   17, 77-78, 82, 86-87, 90, 132
grandfathers   77-78, 86-87, 132
grandmothers – love   17, 82-83, 90, 132
grandmothers – grief   83, 90
GDP   40
genitalia   10, 20, 93, 99, 135
gold medalists   45
good looking   100
grandmaternal love   17, 82-83, 90, 132
grandmaternal grief   83, 90

mid-life crisis   5, 26, 38, 43, 120, 123

Mini Cooper cars   84

misfortune   55, 75, 138

mistake, mistakenly, mistakes   5, 9, 25, 35-36, 43, 53-60, 78-82, 84-85, 126, 130, 132-33

monogynic love   6-10, 13-14, 16-17, 19-21, 25, 77, 86, 88, 91-92, 96, 115, 128-32, 137

monogynic grief   91

morals   109

muscular men   100

music   24

narrow waist   93-94

national happiness   40

new social circles   6, 11, 132

nipple pleasure – men   92, 99

nipple pleasure – women   99-100

novel women   95, 130, 135

novel scenery   102, 104-5, 133

nursing graduates   33

obesity   85, 101, 106-7, 134

offenders   41-42

optimal punishment   62

orgasm – clitoral   99-100, 136

orgasm – penile   92, 95, 99, 136

orgasm – vaginal   99, 136

Olympic gold medalists   45

Oscar winners   30

pain   109

pass the salt   45

parents   8, 26, 34, 48-49, 59, 62-63, 77-78, 84, 86, 88

parental emotions   114, 132

paternal love   84

penile   18, 92, 95, 99, 136

peer, peers   5, 12, 27, 48-52, 60, 138

per capital GDP   40

Notes

About The Author

I am an outsider to psychology. I do not have education or training in psychology or related fields. However, this outsider status allowed me to think outside the box and make the breakthrough insights provided in this book.

I am a management consultant. I was first exposed to evolutionary theory as part of an MBA course at Harvard. That exposure left me with the belief that each of our emotions must have evolved for a unique purpose.

I reasoned that if I could identify an emotion's purpose, I could identify its trigger and vice versa. Following that thought I wrote *The Origin of Emotions* which identifies each emotion's purpose, trigger and effect. Later, I wrote *Happiness Dissected* to provide a more practical and user-friendly exploration of the emotions.

Surprisingly, this breakdown of the emotions based on their purpose has not been done before. One reason is that many emotions are group adaptations – which are not considered possible by mainstream evolutionary academics. They don't believe we can evolve group adaptations, like group emotions, that cause you to harm yourself <u>and your genes</u> to help your group. My outsider status made it easier for me to see that group emotions do exist – revenge being the best example.

Please contact me if you have questions. I am keen to spread the ideas presented in my books. You can reach me at: email@markdevon.com.

www.happinessdissected.com

www.theoriginofemotions.com